123

MASTER YUNMEN

■ ■ ■

MASTER YUNMEN

■ ■ ■

From the Record of the Chan Master "Gate of the Clouds"

■ ■ ■

Translated, edited, and with an introduction by

URS APP

KODANSHA INTERNATIONAL
New York • Tokyo • London

Kodansha America, Inc.
114 Fifth Avenue, New York, NY 10011, U.S.A.

Kodansha International Ltd.
17-14 Otowa 1-chome, Bunkyo-ku, Tokyo 112 Japan

Published in 1994 by Kodansha America, Inc.

Printed in the United States of America

94 95 96 97 98 6 5 4 3 2 1

Library of Congress Cataloging-in-Publication Data
App, Urs, 1949–
Master Yunmen : from the record of the Chan Master "Gate of the
Clouds" / Urs App.
p.   cm.
ISBN 1-56836-004-5/ISBN 1-56836-005-3 (pbk.)
1. Yun-men, 864-949.   2. Zen Buddhism—Doctrines.   I. Yun-men,
864-949 Works Selections 1994.   II. Title.
BQ998.U59A67   1994
294.3'927'092—dc20
[B]   93-42824
CIP

Book design by Laura Hough
The text of this book was set in Bembo.
Printed and bound by R. R. Donnelly & Sons Company,
Harrisonburg, Virginia.

To Yoshitaka Iriya

Contents

■ ■ ■

List of Illustrations and Tables   ix

Preface   xi

INTRODUCTION

A Brief History of Chan   3

The Life of Master Yunmen   17

The Teaching of Master Yunmen   33

TALKS AND DIALOGUES

Corresponding to the Occasion (Nos. 1–144)   83

Essential Sayings from
the Master's Room (Nos. 145–221)   156

Statements With Answers in Place of
the Audience (Nos. 222–263)   197

Critical Examinations (Nos. 264–277)   212

Pilgrimage Record (Nos. 278–285)   220

Contents

MATERIALS

Major Sources for Yunmen's Life and Teaching   229

The History of the *Record of Yunmen*   232

Overview of the Contents of the
Record of Yunmen   239

Yunmen-Related Koans   242

Selective Bibliography   246

List of Illustrations and Tables

■ ■ ■

Photograph of the monastery at Mt. Yunmen, 1990   xiii
Wood-block print of a preface to the *Record*   xix
The outer gate to the Yunmen monastery   6
Overview of Chan in history   7
Historical map with Yunmen's itinerary   16
The mummy of Master Yunmen (1928 photo)   30
The replica of the mummy (1990 photo)   32
Calligraphy   47
Photograph of a stream on Mt. Yunmen and poem   80
Calligraphy   238
Important koans featuring Yunmen   243

Preface

■ ■ ■

Journey to Mt. Yunmen

In the summer of 1990 I made a pilgrimage to the monastery at the foot of Mt. Gate-of-the-Clouds (Mt. Yunmen) in Southern China, the place where Chan Master Yunmen taught slightly more than a thousand years ago. After a seven-hour train ride north from China's southernmost metropolis, Guangzhou (Canton), I arrived after midnight in the city of Shaoguan—one hundred years ago an outpost feared by Wesleyan missionaries because of its hot and humid climate and rampant disease but today just another dusty provincial city. The next morning a bus took me about twenty-five miles westward to a town called Ruyuan ("Source of Milk"), a small settlement in the free zone of the Yao people, a dark-skinned ethnic minority whose striking blue-and-purple costumes appear exotic even to most Chinese. A deep blue river wound its way through this town, and above its tree-lined market streets rose mountains, majestic and green throughout the year. From the bus station I walked north on a sand-covered road glimmering in the midsummer heat. Making my way through a pretty valley dotted with rice fields and banana orchards, I encountered only a few people: a boy guiding a water buffalo, a peasant killing a snake at a roadside well, and a group of herdsmen taking a siesta on a meadow.

Preface

After I had walked for two hours, the valley expanded across a pass into a broad, spectacular plain flanked on the right by a series of mountains—cascades of bold curves shimmering in ever more subtle shades of green and gray under the blinding midday sun. Due to the consistently warm climate, the entire plain was a single magnificent mosaic of rice terraces in all stages of cultivation. These squares of green, brown, and yellow were separated from one another by rows of banana trees waving their huge leaves lazily in the humid heat and by patches of swamp adorned with majestic lotus flowers.

On the left this picturesque plain was overshadowed by a densely overgrown mountain shooting upward in spurts: Mt. Gate-of-the-Clouds or, in Chinese, Yunmen-shan. A little over one thousand years ago this mountain had housed the Chan master called Wenyan who became famous under its name: the master of Mt. Yunmen. Born in 864 near Shanghai, he had come to this region when he was just about sixty years old, and, at the foot of the mountain, had founded the monastery whose long yellow facade I saw glowing under thousands of green roof tiles.

Today's monastery buildings were mostly built during the last ten years. This large construction project was initiated by the present abbot of the monastery and partly financed by the regional government, which is interested in the monastery not only as a cultural site but also as an attraction for Chinese and foreign tourists alike. After entering the walled-in monastery compound through an outer gate, a visitor first finds himself in a courtyard with a curved pond. A long, two-story building, whose yellow facade I had glimpsed earlier, sits on one side of the courtyard. An open gallery at its center leads through to the main monastery grounds. There one is faced with a maze of tree-lined courts and buildings of various sizes, dominated by the massive Buddha Hall where sutra-chanting and religious cere-

The new main facade of Yunmen's monastery (summer of 1990)

monies take place every morning and evening. Behind it is the founder's hall which used to house the mummy of Master Yunmen. The mummy disappeared during the Cultural Revolution, and a wooden replica now takes its place. The meditation hall at the back of the monastery is comparatively small. It appears to be little used outside the two traditional three-month periods of intensive meditation that take place every year. The monastery also has spacious rooms for study, a small library, and a kitchen and dining hall of impressive size. At present, the monastery is home to about eighty monks living, unlike Japanese Zen monks who are housed in large halls, in small individual rooms. They follow a strict schedule of prayer, religious ceremony, and work. The monastery also houses the scores of workers who are still busy with construction. Forty nuns occupying the nearby brand-new nunnery help to run the monastery and participate in the daily ritual.

The square monastery grounds are enveloped towards the mountainside by rows of trees planted by the last famous Chan master who resided here, Xuyun ("Empty Cloud," 1858–1959); he is buried where they meet at the back of the monastery. From that point, a narrow and newly paved path leads into a steep gorge overgrown with luxurious green trees and plants that is filled with the perfumes of exotic flowers and the insistent droning of several kinds of cicadas. Playing hide-and-seek with a rushing brook, the path winds uphill until it ends at the foot of a waterfall, next to an oval pool overlooked by a small hexagonal pavilion. Those prepared to climb can reach two more waterfalls farther up the gorge.

Although the monastery at Mt. Gate-of-the-Clouds is now waking up to renewed greatness it underwent many centuries of neglect and decay. When the great Japanese researcher of Buddhism Daijō Tokiwa visited it in 1927, it consisted only of a few dilapidated buildings. In his report, the great scholar complained that the one remaining monk did not have the slightest idea of its great history and could not even name the master who had founded it. In addition to discovering the mummy of Master Yunmen and some door plates, Professor Tokiwa stumbled on two other very important remnants of the monastery's illustrious past: two stone slabs, or stelae, each the size of a man, standing abandoned in a corner. Engraved on these stelae, which have since been set into the monastery court's walls, are inscriptions dating from 959 and 964 (ten and fifteen years after Yunmen's death). They are the most important sources for Yunmen's biography and also describe the original appearance of the monastery:

> It has many buildings, like clouds forming on all sides. Like
> a palace, it has a penthouse, pillars, soaring eaves, upper

and lower galleries, deep gutters, murmuring springs, and door and window openings which break the summer heat and let cool air enter. Big pine trees and tall bamboos emit their scent and mingle their sounds in harmony. In close to thirty years the assembly counted never less than half a thousand [persons]. (Stone inscription of the year 959)

When the reconstruction of the monastery started around 1985, the end of my second long stay in Japan was already approaching. Three years of that stay had been devoted to research on Master Yunmen and his teachings, which formed the subject of my dissertation. The subsequent writing in my native Switzerland of that first book-length study of the master and his teachings ran, without my knowledge, almost parallel to the construction work at Mt. Yunmen. However, unlike the architects and construction workers who had no idea what the original buildings even looked like, I was lucky to have access to ancient and relatively reliable sources.

The stone inscriptions of 959 and 964 constitute, together with the *Record of Yunmen,* the most important sources of information about the life and teaching of the master (see descriptions in the Materials section). The Introduction following this Preface contains a concise biography of Yunmen that is based on these and other important Chinese sources, as well as a brief history of Chan and a discussion of Chan teaching.

In the main body of the book, I have translated many of Yunmen's talks and dialogues for the first time. The length of the *Record of Yunmen* necessitated a stringent process of selection; I chose to translate all of the longer talks and a representative sample of the hundreds of short dialogues that the *Record* contains. All dialogues used in the four major Chinese koan collections are included (see table, p. 243). Since the first volume of the *Record* appears to be the oldest and most reliable, I decided to cull from it more than half of the total volume of translated parts.

Preface

In the final portion of this book, Materials, the history of the *Record* is traced and an overview of its contents given. Additionally, Yunmen's dialogues that appear as koans in the four major koan collections as well as relevant literature are listed.

This is the place to express my gratitude to my Japanese and American teachers (without, of course, implicating them in the shortcomings that a pioneering effort must entail): to my teacher Yoshitaka Iriya, the man on this globe who is most familiar with the language of Chan texts and whose years of lectures and many afternoons of selfless help have made him a grandparent of this book; to Seizan Yanagida, the director of my research institution, an exemplary Zen researcher and inspiring man; and finally to Richard DeMartino, whose clear sight has opened for me more perspectives than I can recount. I encourage readers interested in my discussion of Yunmen's teaching to read the deeper and more extensive analyses of Zen teaching found in DeMartino's writings (see Selective Bibliography). My thanks also go to friends, colleagues, and students who have read the manuscript or parts of it and helped me in various other ways. I am especially indebted to my editors at Kodansha; to Professors Burton Watson, Victor Mair, and Steven Antinoff; and to Lee Roser, Stephan Schuhmacher, and Wendi Adamek.

I would like to remind Sinologists, Japanologists, scholars of Buddhism, and other specialists that a separate scholarly edition will be published by the Kuroda Institute. It will not include the introductory part of this volume and will feature a very different set of footnotes geared to the needs and interests of specialists and translators. It will also contain, in addition to the Chinese text of all translated passages, an annotated translation of relevant parts of the oldest stone inscription, a translation of prefaces to the text, a more detailed account of the history of the *Record of Yunmen,* extensive lists of biographical and textual sources, various tables that relate the *Record of Yunmen* to other

Preface

Chan texts and inscriptions, indices, and a more comprehensive bibliography.

Note to Text and Translation

This is a partial translation of the *Record of Yunmen*. The full title of the original text is *Yunmen kuangzhen chanshi guanglu* (Comprehensive Records of Chan Master Kuangzhen of Yunmen). To keep matters simple, all editions of this text will be referred to as *Record of Yunmen*. This translation contains approximately one fourth of the volume of the original text. All longer talks by the master, and all koans featuring Yunmen contained in the major koan collections, have been translated. Most of the translated material stems from the oldest parts of the *Record of Yunmen*.

The text used for the translation is found as part of the *Guzunsu yulu* (Record of the Sayings of Old Worthies) in Taiwan's National Central Library in Taipei. This oldest extant edition of the *Record of Yunmen* dates from the year 1267.

Because this Taipei edition is not available to most scholars and students, I decided to key all references to an edition found in many libraries in East and West, namely, that contained in volume 47 of the Taishō edition of the Chinese Buddhist canon.[1] Other texts contained in this largest collection of Chinese Buddhist texts (for example, the *Record of Linji* and the *Blue Cliff Record*) are also cited in the following standard format: T (standing for Taishō), followed by volume, page, section, and line identification (e.g., T47: 545b15 for Taishō canon volume 47, p. 545, section b, line 15). The abbreviation ZZ stands for the Japanese Zokuzōkyō collection of Chinese Buddhist texts.

The original Chinese text indicates the beginning of con-

---

[1] See the Materials section for more detail.

versations or formal talks by spaces. For more convenient cross-reference and identification, I gave each translated section a number.

I strove to make the translation as literal as possible while conveying the flavor and style of the original. In general, words that in my opinion are implied in the terse Chinese text were put in square brackets.[1] Since such additions often affect the overall meaning of the text, I judged it necessary to identify them as my own and thus give the reader the option of ignoring everything in brackets. Words in parentheses have been added to convey equivalent terms with which some readers might be more familiar.[2] The original Chinese text contains neither brackets nor parentheses.

---

[1] For example: "[You must be hungry after such a long trip;] there's gruel and rice on the long bench!" (section 104).

[2] Thus I have, for example, translated the Chinese *fa* as "separate entity (dharma)."

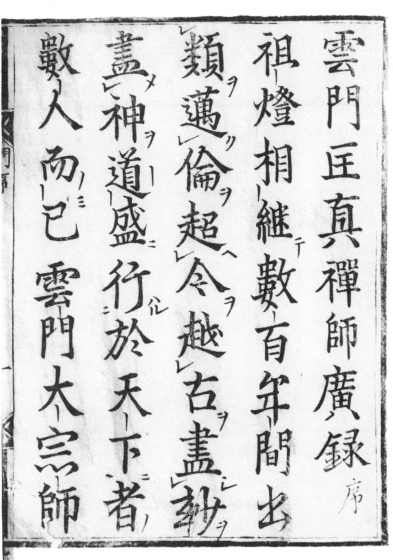

雲門匡真禪師廣録序

祖燈相繼數百年間出類邁倫超令越古盡妙盡神道盛行於天下者數人而已雲門大宗師

Japanese wood-block print of a preface to the Record of Yunmen

Introduction

A Brief History
of Chan

■ ■ ■

Setting the Stage for Chan

Long before Buddhism arrived in China around the beginning of
the common era, Chinese thinkers taught ideas whose orientation was of striking similarity to some central tenets of that foreign religion that had yet to arrive. These teachings, ascribed to
the ancient sages Laozi (Lao-tzu) and Zhuangzi (Chuang-tzu),
are often called "philosophical Daoism," and originated in China
between the fourth and second centuries before the common era.
They not only contain a fundamental expression of the wisdom
of the Chinese and their view of humanity—its beauty, its prob-
lematic sides, and its ideals—but are also great works of literary art
whose imagery and terminology exerted an unmistakable influence on later religious and philosophical teachings. In particular,
the writings of Zhuangzi, the author of parts of a classic of the
same name,[1] and of his followers were to play an important role in
facilitating the introduction and acculturation of Buddhism in
China some centuries later. Many of Zhuangzi's stories exude a

---

[1] Burton Watson, *The Complete Works of Chuang Tzu* (New York: Columbia
University Press, 1968). A more recent and more selective translation, which
also discusses the question of authorship, was published by A. C. Graham:
Chuang-tzu: The Inner Chapters (London: George Allen & Unwin, 1981).

kind of down-to-earth spirituality which is very similar to that found a thousand years later in Chan texts. For example:

> Duke Huan was in his hall reading a book. The wheel-wright P'ien, who was in the yard below chiseling a wheel, laid down his mallet and chisel, stepped up into the hall, and said to Duke Huan, "This book Your Grace is reading—may I venture to ask whose words are in it?"
>
> "The words of sages," said the duke.
>
> "Are the sages still alive?"
>
> "Dead long ago," said the duke.
>
> "In that case, what you are reading there is nothing but the chaff and dregs of the men of old!"
>
> "Since when does a wheelwright have permission to comment on the books I read?" said Duke Huan. "If you have some explanation, well and good. If not, it's your life!"
>
> Wheelwright P'ien said, "I look at it from the point of view of my own work. When I chisel a wheel, if the blows of the mallet are too gentle, the chisel slides and won't take hold. But if they're too hard, it bites in and won't budge. Not too gentle, not too hard—you can get it in your hand and feel it in your mind. You can't put it into words, and yet there's a knack to it somehow. I can't teach it to my son, and he can't learn it from me. So I've gone along for seventy years and at my age I'm still chiseling wheels. When the men of old died, they took with them the things that couldn't be handed down. So what you are reading there must be nothing but the chaff and the dregs of the men of old."[1]

---

[1] The translation is by Burton Watson, *Chuang Tzu,* pp. 152–53. Graham (1981, p. 257) classifies this chapter under the syncretist writings, probably authored in the second century B.C.

Such currents of thought had already existed in China for several centuries when Buddhism was gradually imported to China by people traveling the silk road. As in many other religions, images or icons initially played a much more important role than texts written in foreign languages. However, beginning in the third century, an increasing number of Sanskrit Buddhist scriptures were translated into Chinese. These translations made ample use of terms coined by Zhuangzi and Laozi as well as by their heirs and commentators. The translation process, however, was not limited to the words in scriptures. Rather, the whole Indian religion was given a Chinese face, not unlike the Buddha statues whose facial features gradually changed from Indo-European large noses and eyes to their Chinese equivalents. By the sixth century there were already several forms of Buddhism that were unmistakably Chinese in character. Among them was the fledgling movement that will primarily concern us here: Chan Buddhism.

Chinese Buddhist Meditation

The Chan movement did not shoot out of the Chinese ground like a bamboo stalk during the rainy season; rather, it grew gradually from soil that had been formed during centuries of extensive adaptation of doctrine and practice to the conditions of China. In the first few centuries, Chinese Buddhist nuns and monks engaged in activities such as building monasteries, performing rituals, copying and translating texts, studying Buddhist doctrine and rules of monastic discipline, and performing feats of magic. Meditation was also an important part of Chinese Buddhism from an early period, and several noted teachers and movements placed a strong emphasis on meditative concentration. The Sanskrit term for such concentration was dhyāna; imitating the sound of this word, the Chinese called it "Chan." The eminent scholar-monk Daoan (312–385), for instance, outlined

The author at the outer gate to Yunmen's monastery (1990)

in one of his prefaces the meditative process that leads from the counting of breaths to a state of pure awareness. The early and extensive popularity of meditation practices was in part due to the belief that through such practices various magical powers could be acquired. Thus, centuries before we can discern the movement we now label Chan Buddhism, there were numerous monks with meditative ("Chan") interests gathering around teachers who appeared to have actualized what the texts explain and who concentrated their efforts on leading their students in the same direction.

Era	Century	Event
B.C.E. (B.C.)	6TH–5TH	Confucius establishes an important current in Chinese thought which later also becomes a religion. Roughly at the same time, the Buddha lays through his teaching the foundation for the Buddhist religion.
	4TH–2ND	The books attributed to Zhuangzi and Laozi are authored and form the focal point of Daoist philosophical thought.
C.E. (A.D.)	1ST–2ND	Buddhism is introduced in China by traders on the silk road. Images play an important role.
	2ND–3RD	First official records of Buddhism in China. First translations of Sanskrit texts into Chinese.
	3RD–6TH	Thorough acculturation of the Indian religion in China. Many texts are translated into Chinese, using Daoist terminology. The religion gets an increasingly Chinese character. Meditation is of major importance.
	6TH–8TH	Early Chan becomes distinguishable from similar groupings that emphasize meditation. Various doctrinal debates take place. Early Chan gains influence in Tibet and Korea (Son).
	8TH–10TH	Classical Chan: the age of the great masters, which influenced all later teaching: Zhaozhou (Jōshū), Linji (Rinzai), etc. Master Yunmen may be the last great master of the classical age. Sayings of the masters are collected.
	10TH–13TH	Song Chan: Chan becomes a major religious and cultural force in China. Classical sayings are edited, become the subject of commentaries, and are published. The koan arises as a teaching and practicing device. Chan is introduced to Japan (Zen) and gains wider influence from the 13th century (Eisai, Dōgen).
	13TH–19TH	Yuan, Ming, and Qing Chan: Chan is a dominant force in Chinese and Korean Buddhism. In Japan, the Rinzai and Sōtō Zen traditions develop a distinctive character and have considerable cultural influence.
	20TH	Japanese Zen (and later Korean Son and Chinese Chan) are introduced to the West, where many centers form.

Overview of Chan in history

Early Chan

After the adaptation and translation phase of Indian Buddhism in China (second to fifth centuries) and the gradual formation of meditative circles belonging to various schools of Chinese Buddhism, the movement we now call Chan emerges as an identifiable entity around the sixth century of the common era. Stories by later authors assert that the Chan tradition had been founded in the fifth or sixth century by the Indian monk Bodhidharma, whose teachings are said to have been handed down through a succession of patriarchs to the sixth and most famous one: Huineng, the purported author of the *Platform Sutra*.[1] Recent research shows that the early phase of Chan did not proceed as smoothly as later authors would make us believe; rather, it appears as a period marked by numerous controversies of doctrinal and personal nature. The best known of these disputes divided Chan adherents in the so-called Northern ("gradual awakening") and Southern ("immediate awakening") factions. Some themes that were discussed gained broader attention; the gradual/immediate controversy, for example, stood also at the center of the "Council of Tibet," a famous public controversy at the end of the eighth century involving representatives of early Chinese Chan and Indian Buddhism.

Professor Seizan Yanagida, who after World War II almost single-handedly rewrote the history of early Chan, has pointed out that masters in the sixth to eighth centuries still discussed the nature of Buddhist awakening much in the words of the sutras or holy scriptures of Buddhism—scriptures that were thought to reproduce the actual words of the historical Buddha. But gradu-

---

[1] This text was translated into English and studied by Philip Yampolsky: *The Platform Sutra of the Sixth Patriarch* (New York: Columbia University Press, 1967).

ally more and more importance was given to the words of Chinese masters who had realized the spirit of these scriptures in themselves—people who had themselves become buddhas, or "awakened ones."[1] These masters used simple words to explain the essence of awakening and responded in like manner to concrete questions about its realization.[2]

Although the Chan movement did not yet have a clearly discernible monastic organization, its teachings and teaching methods became remarkably different from those of other sects. The widespread emergence of illustrious and original Chan teachers marks the onset of the classical age of Chan (eighth to tenth centuries), to which Yunmen belongs.

The Classical Age of Chan

Around the end of the eighth century a number of masters taught what they took to be the essence of Buddhism in a startlingly direct and fresh way. In examining the sources we have from this period, we notice an extraordinary change in the way masters related to their students and vice versa. Suddenly few

---

[1] See Seizan Yanagida, "The 'Recorded Sayings' Texts of Chinese Ch'an Buddhism," in *Early Ch'an in China and Tibet,* ed. Whalen Lai and Lewis R. Lancaster (Berkeley: University of California, 1983).

[2] An early example is a text found in the Dunhuang caves, entitled "On the Extinction of Views," translated into English by Gishin Tokiwa, *A Dialogue on the Contemplation-Extinguished* (Kyoto: The Institute for Zen Studies, 1973). There is also a translation with comments by the modern Japanese Zen master Morinaga in his *A Treatise on the Ceasing of Notions,* trans. Ursula Jarand (London: The Zen Centre, 1988). The Dunhuang caves, situated in China's Far West on the Silk Road, were discovered in the early twentieth century. They contained, apart from many paintings, thousands of manuscripts and various other materials. Several early Chan texts of great importance for the study of the history of this movement were found among the manuscripts.

quotes from scriptures appeared in talks by these masters; instead of repeating the words of the historically remote Buddha or commenting on them, these masters *themselves* spoke, here and now—and they are not beyond whacking and swearing if the need arises. In place of doctrinal hairsplitting, they demonstrate the teachings in action, shouting and joking, telling stories, and handing out abuse or encouragement as they see fit. The unctuous style of Buddhist sermons gives way to colloquialisms and slang: the masters of the classic age of Chan talk so bluntly that to some people, such as the Japanese pilgrim Ennin, their talks must at the outset have been hardly identifiable as Buddhist.

Instead of learned discussions about this or that doctrinal problem of the past, the masters and their students drive directly at the one thing they consider essential: being a *buddha* oneself, right here and now. In the following example from a classical Chan record, we see Master Linji simply repeating a question of a student, whereupon the student resorts to a physical action that seeks to show that the master is not really an awakened teacher. However, the master quickly gets the better of the questioner. Characteristically, he does this not by asking him a complicated question about Buddhist doctrine but rather by a completely unexpected inquiry about the questioner's well-being:

> One day Lin-chi went to Ho-fu. Counselor Wang the Prefectural Governor requested the Master to take the high seat. At that time Ma-yü came forward and asked, "The Great Compassionate One has a thousand hands and a thousand eyes. Which is the true eye?" The Master said: "The Great Compassionate One has a thousand hands and a thousand eyes. Which is the true eye? Speak, speak!" Ma-yü pulled the Master down off the high seat and sat on it himself. Coming up to him, the Master said: "How are you doing?" Ma-yü hesitated. The Master, in his turn,

pulled Ma-yü off the high seat and sat upon it himself.
Ma-yü went out. The Master stepped down.[1]

Most of what we know about the teachings of this classic
age of Chan stems from later compendia containing biographies
and samples of teachings and from the collected sayings of various masters. Such sayings were often recorded by the masters'
disciples and went through the hands of a number of compilers
and editors. The instructions and dialogues that are translated in
this volume come from a typical example of the "recorded sayings"[2] genre, the *Record of Yunmen*.

The great majority of Chan's most famous masters, including Mazu, Linji, and Zhaozhou, lived during the two centuries
before the turn of the millennium. Master Yunmen is the last
Chan teacher of this classical period who rose to great fame.
These teachers and their disciples form the classic core of the
Chan tradition within the whole of Chinese Buddhism. The
records and compendia of this time are also classic in the sense
that they functioned as both the main source and the reference
point of Chan teaching ever since, even in Korea, Japan, and
now the West. Today's Chan, Son, and Zen masters constantly
refer to their classic Chinese forebears, and much of the writing
about Chan consists—like this book—of translations of the sayings of classical masters.

Collections of the words of masters were treated as prize
possessions as early as the ninth century. But this very adulation
of old writings was criticized by many masters. In the *Record of*

---

[1] *Record of Linji*, T47: 496c4–8. Translation taken from Ruth Fuller Sasaki, *The Recorded Sayings of Ch'an Master Lin-chi Hui-chao of Chen Prefecture* (Kyoto: In-stitute for Zen Studies, 1975), p. 2. (Later references to this translation indi-cated by "Sasaki translation.")

[2] Ch. *yulu*, Jap. *goroku*.

Linji (Jap. Rinzai, died 866), for example, we find the following words:

> Students of today get nowhere because they base their un-
> derstanding upon the acknowledgment of names. They
> inscribe the words of some dead old guy in a great big
> notebook, wrap it up in four or five squares of cloth, and
> won't let anyone look at it. "This is the Mysterious Princi-
> ple," they aver, and safeguard it with care. That's all
> wrong. Blind idiots! What kind of juice are you looking
> for in such dried-up bones![1]

Master Linji's harsh criticism of collecting and safeguarding the words of masters points towards the central aim of Chan teaching. Since approximately the year 1000, the following quatrain has been used to characterize Chan:

> *[Chan] is transmitted outside established doctrine;*
> *it does not institute words. [Rather,]*
> *It points directly to the human being's heart:*
> *whoever sees his own nature becomes an awakened*
> > *buddha.*

Because of the role that Chan texts and Buddhist scriptures play at Chan monasteries, the meaning of the first two lines of this quatrain has provoked much discussion. To me, they point to what Kierkegaard once said about the Bible. He said that reading it is like looking at a mirror: some may wonder of what material it is crafted, how much it cost, how it functions, where it comes from, etc. Others, however, look into that mirror to face themselves. It is the latter attitude that is addressed in the quatrain above.

The central concern of Chan is nothing other than the

---

[1] *Record of Linji,* T47: 501c14–17 (Sasaki translation, p. 31).

thorough seeing of one's own nature, and the Buddha and the enlightened masters after him tried to guide and prod their students towards this. Many of these masters point out that with such a goal, sutras as well as Chan scriptures can be no more than a finger pointing at the moon. Yet these very observations were written down and soon collected in records comprising the sayings of individual masters.

In addition to such records, compendia appeared that usually furnished the biographical information and selected teachings of numerous masters. These compendia are another sign of the growing awareness on the part of Chan monks that they were members of a single tradition which could be arranged in various lineages. The first major compendium of this kind is the *Collection from the Founder's Halls* (Ch. Zutangji, Kor. Chodang chip, Jap. Sodōshū), completed in 952. It appeared just three years after Master Yunmen's death and stands at the end of the classical age, just as the second major compendium, the *Jingde Era Record of the Transmission of the Lamp* (Ch. Jingde chuandenglu, Jap. Keitoku dentōroku), published in 1004, marks the beginning of a new period of great expansion and literary and cultural productivity during the Song dynasty (960–1279).

Chan in the Second Millennium

Around the turn of the millennium the first rulers of the Song dynasty ushered in a new political age in which Chan flourished. The religion broadened its influence dramatically and grew into a considerable force both religiously and culturally. During the Song dynasty, the Chan Buddhist not only attracted respect (or criticism) as members of a famous movement, they also created much of what we now call Chan monasticism (monastic rules, rituals, etc.), Chan methodology (especially the systematic use of koans), Chan literature (recorded sayings, koan collections, Chan histories, etc.), and Chan art (painting, calligraphy, etc.).

This influence radiated internationally, as some talented Japanese monks like Eisai and Dōgen studied in China and founded Zen traditions upon their return to Japan.

Although during the classical age lineages were not at all distinct and many monks studied under different masters at different times, the Song editors of compendia and Chan histories made great efforts to reduce the complex historical web to neat linear threads strung from master to successor. Thus they began to speak of five major classical traditions of Chan: those of Guiyang (Jap. Igyō), Linji (Jap. Rinzai), Caodong (Jap. Sōtō), Yunmen (Jap. Ummon), and Fayan (Jap. Hōgen). The two most influential traditions during the Song era were the lines of Yunmen and Linji. This is probably due to both the eminence of their progenitors and the presence in these two lines of literarily gifted monks who rewrote Chan history and edited various compendia, chronicles, and records. The best known representative of the Yunmen line was Xuetou Chongxian (980–1052), the gifted poet and popular Chan teacher who wrote the poetic comments in the *Blue Cliff Record*. Partly because of monks like him, Yunmen overshadows all other masters with regard to the number of his sayings included in Song-era koan collections. All three major koan collections (the *Blue Cliff Record,* the *Gateless Barrier,* and the *Record of Serenity*) feature Yunmen as protagonist more often than any other master.[1]

A representative of the line of Yunmen who was in many ways typical was Master Qisong (1007–1072), who lived four generations after Yunmen. He was the author of a book entitled *Record of the True Tradition of Dharma Transmission,* which tried to show that Chan is the most genuine of the traditions of Bud-

---

[1] See the table on p. 243. The Bibliography lists English translations of these collections under Cleary (1977, 1990, 1993), Yamada (1990), and Shibayama (1974).

dhism. Such texts had considerable influence on the intelligentsia of the time, so much so that the great Neo-Confucianist philosopher Zhuxi (1130–1200) discussed mainly Chan teachings when writing about Buddhism. But this influence went both ways: Master Qisong was also an ardent student of Confucianism and composed a book about one of the four Confucian classics, the *Doctrine of the Mean,* as well as other works that make an argument for the underlying unity of such different teachings.

The Yunmen line flourished for about two centuries after the death of the master. Towards the end of the Song dynasty it was gradually absorbed into the Linji tradition, as were all the other Chan lines with the exception of Caodong (Jap. Sōtō). During the Yuan dynasty (1260–1367), the Yunmen line vanished altogether. From the Ming dynasty (1368–1644) on, the Linji tradition flourished to such an extent that it became practically synonymous in China with Chan and even Buddhism as a whole. By the beginning of the twentieth century to be a Linji monk meant little more than to be an ordained Buddhist monk.

The influence of Yunmen's teaching, however, did not suffer the same fate as his school: it remains omnipresent in Chan to this day. But before examining his teachings in greater depth, let us first take a look at the life of the master.

Historical Map of South China with Yunmen's Itinerary

The Life of
Master Yunmen

■ ■ ■

Youth

Yunmen was born in 864 in Jiaxing, a town between Shanghai and Hangzhou on China's eastern coast. His family name was Zhang; but because it was the custom for Buddhist monks to abandon their family names, he became known as Wenyan and later took the name of Mt. Yunmen, at whose foot he built his monastery. To avoid unnecessary confusion, I will refer to him as Yunmen throughout the text.

Yunmen's birth came at a time of great political upheaval. In the years between 842 and 845, the central government of China had proscribed Buddhism and other "foreign" religions. Several hundred thousand monks and nuns were defrocked and secularized, 4,600 monasteries and 40,000 smaller sanctuaries were destroyed or converted to other uses, and the greater part of monastic property was seized.[1] As the Tang period was drawing to a close, the central government had already lost much of its power, and in some regions of the empire (an area about the size of Europe) that power had virtually disintegrated by the

---

[1] See Jacques Gernet, *A History of Chinese Civilization* (Cambridge and New York: Cambridge University Press, 1982), p. 294 ff.

time of Yunmen's birth. In remote regions Buddhist movements were gaining in vigor and influence and developing ever more idiosyncratic forms of teaching and practice. The most prominent of these movements was Chan.

Before we follow the course of Yunmen's life, a cautionary remark is appropriate: The biographies of religious men in China are, not unlike those of other religions, full of set stories and expressions. Pivotal events in a person's life tend to receive little attention in early sources and ever more detailed descriptions in later ones. It is thus impossible to take all the available information at face value; usually, the best one can do is to rely on early sources and carefully compare all available materials.[1]

Like many other eminent monks, Yunmen is said to have had extraordinary powers of memory. The stone inscription of 964 reports that from birth he showed signs of great intelligence and that as a child he learned poems and entire Buddhist scriptures by heart after a single reading. Yunmen is also said to have been keenly aware of his spiritual leanings and to have decided to take the path of monkhood upon reaching adolescence. According to the biography contained in the *Record of Yunmen,* young Yunmen was also characterized by a strong aversion to vulgarity, a tendency to be exemplary, and great eloquence.

Several sources assert that as a boy Yunmen entered the Kongwang temple of his hometown, where he passed some years studying under a specialist in monastic discipline named Zhi Cheng. While the boy underwent this initial training, the rebellion of Huang Chao (874–883) shook the foundations of the Chinese empire, and both its eastern and southern fringes (the regions where Yunmen grew up and eventually settled

---

[1] The information about Yunmen's life that follows is generally from the earliest available sources; when I mention variations from later sources, I will identify them as such.

down, respectively) gradually achieved autonomy. Various local leaders emerged and took power; in the area near Shanghai that contained Jiaxing, for example, the former bandit leader Qian Lu worked his way up to the position of general (878) and eventually supreme potentate.

Yunmen took the monastic precepts at the usual age of twenty in the town of Changzhou, near beautiful Suzhou, a town not far inland from Shanghai that is famous for its exquisite gardens, romantic canals, and tree-lined boulevards. Afterwards, he returned to Zhi Cheng and concentrated on studying the voluminous monastic rule literature. We are told that he soon started to lecture about monastic discipline. It is not clear how many years Yunmen remained with this first teacher, and since no source gives exact dates for the period between Yunmen's twentieth and thirtieth year, we must be content with approximate dates.

Meeting with Master Muzhou

Around the age of twenty-five Yunmen set out to meet the famous Daozong who was known as "Reverend Chen"[1] and sojourned in Muzhou, about seventy miles upriver from Hangzhou. Unfortunately not much is known about this man; according to the *Transmission of Treasures of Monks of the Chan Tradition* of 1122, he had been (together with Linji/Rinzai) a disciple of the famous Master Huangbo (Jap. Ōbaku). Having left the Mishan monastery at Gaoan in what is now Jiangsi province, Reverend Chen returned home to Muzhou to take care of his aging mother. After a stay at the local Longxing monastery, he left monastic life altogether and supported himself and his

---

[1] This man is known by various names, for example: Muzhou Daozong, Muzhou Daoming, Reverend Chen, and Sandal-Chen.

mother by making sandals. Like many other Chan masters, he became known under the name of the locality where he stayed and thus was also called Master Muzhou. He was noted for his reclusiveness and his abrupt manner; indeed, the records about him consist almost entirely of very short dialogues.

By the time that Yunmen visited him, Muzhou was probably very old. It is said that Yunmen tried on one or more occasions to see the former monk but was turned away. The older stone inscription describes his crucial attempt as follows:[1]

[Master Muzhou's] one room was usually shut, and it was completely empty. When he occasionally did receive people, he allowed no deliberations. When Yunmen could freely roll in and out,[2] he went straight to Muzhou's door and knocked.

Master Muzhou asked, "Who is it?"

Yunmen: "It is me, [Yunmen] Wenyan."

Muzhou blocked the entrance and said, "Why do you keep coming?"

Yunmen replied, "I am not clear about myself."

Muzhou said, "Absolutely useless stuff!,"[3] pushed Yunmen out and shut the door.

In this way Yunmen attained understanding.

---

[1] See section 278 for another portrayal of this encounter.

[2] This expression is in the Chan tradition used for folding all different phenomena into their one uniting principle and inversely for the demonstration of this one principle in the various phenomena. This double ability to show the one in the many and the many in the one is said to characterize an accomplished practitioner.

[3] Literally: "Stone drills from the Qin period." These gigantic drills were fashioned for the construction of a huge palace by the Qin emperor. Since the megalomaniac project was never realized, these tools achieved proverbial status as something that is utterly useless.

The Life of Master Yunmen

Though later sources embellish this story, in the majority of sources its core remains essentially unchanged: the problem which drives Yunmen to seek instruction is not some *thing* that bothers him but rather his own self. This is not one of a number of problems he *has,* but rather the problem he himself *is.*[1] I will come back to this point in the introduction to the master's teaching.

Another common element of the various sources is that Yunmen, having barely formulated his problem, is jolted by an abrupt response from Muzhou and at that moment gains a profound realization. There remains disagreement over various aspects of this encounter, including the number of Yunmen's previous unsuccessful visits and the exact nature of the event that triggered the breakthrough.[2]

Whatever the specifics of the encounter, it resulted in a decisive breakthrough that the sources describe with the vocabulary commonly used for Buddhist awakening: enlightenment, liberation from doubts, perfect match with the core of teachings, realization of the essence of one's own heart-mind and of the great meaning—great awakening, satori.

After this event, Yunmen stayed with Master Muzhou for several years; though we cannot be sure of the exact number of

---

[1] This distinction is made and explained in Richard DeMartino's "The Human Situation and Zen Buddhism," in D. T. Suzuki, Erich Fromm, and Richard DeMartino, *Zen Buddhism and Psychoanalysis* (New York: Harper & Row, 1970), pp. 142–71.

[2] Especially in some later sources the following story is related: Yunmen squeezed inside the master's room, but Muzhou immediately seized him and demanded: "Speak, speak!" Yunmen was flabbergasted, and Muzhou without delay threw him out, muttering "Totally useless stuff!," and shut the door on Yunmen's leg. The resulting sharp pain is in these stories the trigger of Yunmen's breakthrough. A simple account of this course of events first appeared around 160 years after the master's death; it was subsequently told and retold in increasingly colorful detail (for instance, in case 6 of the *Blue Cliff Record*).

years,[1] the similarity of the style and diction between the *Record of Yunmen* and that of Muzhou suggests that Muzhou's influence was deep and lasting.

Encounter with Master Xuefeng; Pilgrimage

Muzhou was fully conscious of his disciple's potential, and after having taught Yunmen for a few years he sent him to the renowned Chan master Xuefeng[2] for further training. Such training after awakening was common and served to prepare future teachers for their task. In general, many teachers were visited over one or more decades, in the course of which teaching skills were gradually honed and experience was gained.

In the case of Yunmen, this training lasted for seventeen years and began around his thirtieth year with the visit to Xuefeng. This master was living in the Kingdom of Min on the coast opposite the island of Taiwan. This region, which corresponds roughly to today's Fujian province, had become rather wealthy through sea trade and was quick to assume independence when the authority of the central government waned. Thanks to the strong interest in Buddhism shown by the potentate Wang Shenzhi (a good friend of Master Xuefeng), several large monasteries were being built or restored around the time of Yunmen's arrival. Master Xuefeng taught at the monastic community of the Snow Peak (Xuefeng) temple on Mt. Elephant Bone, which was said to have been home to more than a thousand monks. The proverbial expression "In the north Master

---

[1] The *Record of Xuefeng* (which is not beyond suspicion when it comes to such matters) states that Yunmen stayed three years with Muzhou and lived during this time at the home of a lay disciple of Muzhou, the magistrate Chen Cao (ZZ119: 482c18).

[2] Xuefeng Yicun (822–908).

The Life of Master Yunmen

Zhaozhou,[1] in the south Master Xuefeng"[2] suggests just how famous Master Xuefeng must have been.

The story of the meeting of Yunmen and Xuefeng fired the imagination of many a writer, but again we will try to stay close to the earlier stone inscription—which, incidentally, agrees here with the *Collection from the Founder's Halls,* the important early Chan history compiled in circles around Xuefeng before 952:

> Master [Yunmen] thus went to Min. Hardly had he climbed Mt. Elephant Bone than he already demonstrated his immeasurable ability: When he reached Xuefeng's assembly and the threefold salutation was about to be performed, Xuefeng said, "How could it come to this?" Master [Yunmen] did not move one hair's breadth and impressively demonstrated his complete ability. But although he had cut through the stream [of deluded consciousness] he also carried horns [like the deluded ones]. So none of the more than 1000 students [of Xuefeng] knew for sure whether he was an ordinary or a holy man. For many cold and hot seasons, Yunmen went to question [Xuefeng] at dusk and dawn.

This account intends to point out that when he went to meet Master Xuefeng, Yunmen already had great ability but did not wish to show it off. Section 279 of this volume furnishes an embroidered version of this meeting and shows how editors added much detail to such stories.

It is certain that Yunmen spent a number of years with Xuefeng, although it is impossible to know exactly how many.

---

[1] Zhaozhou Congshen (778–897). This master was in his time—and tradition makes it a rather long time—probably the most celebrated Chan teacher.

[2] See sections 86 and 134 of this book.

In view of the long journey that followed the stay at Mt. Elephant Bone, it seems likely that Yunmen left in his late thirties and spent ten more years on pilgrimage before he settled down in China's deep south at the age of forty-seven. I will not trace all of his movements during this journey (see map on p. 16); suffice it to say that Yunmen visited and interviewed many masters[1] before, in 911, visiting the temple in South China where the Sixth Patriarch Huineng is said to have stayed. It was in this region with its long Chan tradition that Yunmen was destined to begin his active life as a Chan teacher.

Arrival in South China

Like Min, the southernmost region in the Chinese empire (which included the coastal stretches around Hong Kong and the Cantonese hinterland) reached comparative wealth through sea trade and inched towards autonomy as soon as central power faltered. Liu Yin, a man from the Min region, had moved to the Canton (Guangzhou) region and made a name for himself after 878 as a fighter loyal to the central government in its fight against the rebel Huang Chao. While the central government gave him a succession of increasingly lofty titles, he brought the whole region under his power. He died the same year Yunmen arrived in this region, and the younger brother who succeeded him, Liu Yan, later became Yunmen's most important sponsor.

After visiting the pilgrimage site connected with the Sixth

---

[1] It may be noteworthy that Yunmen visited a number of successors of Dongshan Liangjie (Jap. Tōzan Ryōkai; 807–869), one of the founders of the Caodong/Sōtō lineage of Zen. The second father of that lineage, Caoshan Benji (Jap. Sōzan Honjaku; 840–901), is also among them. Disciples of Xuefeng and Yunmen's co-disciple Xuansha Shibei are also well represented. Some of these dialogues are translated in this volume.

Patriarch, Yunmen traveled to the nearby city of Shaoguan and met with Master Rumin of Lingshu, who headed a community of monks. Old sources simply state that the two hit it off well and formed a deep friendship. Later sources emphasize, as biographies of Chinese monks often do, Rumin's spiritual powers and tell us that Rumin had known all along that Yunmen would visit and when. Even more recent sources state that Rumin intuited the exact time of Yunmen's arrival and sent his monks to greet him.[1] At any rate, Yunmen became the head monk in Master Rumin's monastery and served in this capacity until Rumin's death seven years later. It is reported that, before he died, Rumin foresaw an impending imperial visit to his temple. Liu Yan (who had given himself the name of Emperor Gaozu) did indeed come to the Lingshu monastery soon after Rumin's death in 918, and gave orders to cremate the master's body and to fashion a statue in his likeness. Liu Yan first met head monk Yunmen during this visit.

After succeeding his brother in 911, Liu Yan, no longer content with the ever more bombastic titles that the central government had been conferring on him to keep him subservient, had in the year 915 stopped all financial contributions. Two years later he elevated himself formally to the post which he in fact already occupied: that of supreme ruler of his own empire, which he first named Great Yue and later Southern Han. After Rumin's death, Yunmen was summoned for an audience with the emperor, who honored him with the purple robe, a governmental decoration reserved for eminent monks. One year later,

---

[1] Such increasingly detailed descriptions often provide clues as to the dating of biographies or elements thereof; in this case, the rich detail of this episode as told in the biography contained in the *Record of Yunmen*—which is dated very soon after Yunmen's death—indicates that this biography probably was "improved upon" by some later editor.

in 919, the emperor named the fifty-five-year-old Yunmen abbot of Lingshu monastery. This was the official beginning of thirty years of uninterrupted teaching for Yunmen.

Teaching

For a few years, Yunmen taught in the Lingshu monastery in Shaoguan, but the monastery's steady stream of visitors soon became too distracting for him and his students. The stone inscriptions tell us:

> Master Yunmen got tired of receiving and entertaining people and wished to reside at a remote and pure place. He turned to the emperor with a request to change his place of residence. He got the imperial permission, and in the twentieth year of the sixty-year cycle (923), Yunmen ordered his disciples to open up Mt. Yunmen for construction. Five years later, the work was completed.

So, at the age of sixty-four, Yunmen found the quiet place where he would teach monks and lay disciples for another two decades. Most of the talks and dialogues contained in the *Record of Yunmen* presumably come from this twenty-year period. Here the master had a stable monastic setting and a community that included those who took down notes from his talks and thus laid the basis of the text that is partly translated in this volume. Furthermore, Yunmen enjoyed the full support of emperor Liu Yan, who had himself brushed the characters "Chan monastery of Enlightened Peace" on the monastery's large door plate. The inscription of 959 tells the following story about Yunmen's dealings with Liu Yan:

> In the thirty-fifth year (938) His Heavenly Majesty the Great Emperor Gaozu (Liu Yan) summoned Master [Yunmen] to the Imperial Palace [for an audience]. The em-

peror asked, "What is Chan all about?" Master [Yunmen] said, "Your Majesty has the question, and your servant the monk has the answer."[1]

The emperor inquired, "What answer?" Master [Yunmen] replied, "I request Your Majesty to reflect upon the words your servant has just uttered." The emperor was pleased and said: "I know your personal precept, and I have respected it early." He decreed that the office of Inspector of the Monks of the Capital be given to Master [Yunmen]. The Master remained silent and did not respond.

Coming back to this decree, an imperial advisor said, "This Master has completed his training and knows the path; he is not likely to enjoy rising to a high post." The emperor then said, "Shall we let you return to your mountain?" Master [Yunmen] full of joy shouted thrice "Long live the emperor!" The following day Master [Yunmen] was presented with goods from the treasury, incense, and medicinal herbs, and he received donations of salt and other goods. When Master [Yunmen] returned to his mountain, [the emperor] conferred along with all this the title "Genuine Truth" upon him. Following this [His Majesty] made donations several times every year; these donations were often not duly recorded.

---

[1] A passage in the early Zen text *About the Extinction of Contemplation* (section 15, paragraph 3) reads:

> [The student of the Way] asked, "The ordinary being, because of what he is, asks questions; the Most Honored One, because of what he is, preaches. [Is this so?]"
>
> [The Master] answered, "Because of the doubt one has, one asks. So as to remove the doubt one preaches."

For English translations of this text see the Bibliography (Gishin Tokiwa, Morinaga).

Yunmen's good relations with the imperial court were maintained beyond the death of Liu Yan in 942 and the murder of his successor one year later. The next emperor, who called himself Zhongzong, invited Yunmen to the imperial palace for one month and gave him many presents, including an imperial inscription for the master's grave. But although Yunmen was already seventy-nine, he taught at the foot of Mt. Gate-of-the-Clouds for a few more years before making use of this gift.

Death of the Master

On May 10, 949, the eighty-five-year-old master suddenly had no more appetite and slept less. The earlier stone inscription gives the following account about his death:

> When his attendant offered him a hot [medical] broth, the Master handed the bowl back and said, "First, I am fine; second, you are fine! Be sure to write a letter to request my leave from the emperor." And then he wrote himself a document with his admonitions for posterity which went: "After my death I permit neither the wearing of mourning clothes in conformity with worldly custom nor wailing and holding a ceremony with a funeral carriage. This would be a violation of the Buddha's precepts and a source of trouble for the Chan school." He transmitted the Dharma to Zhixiang [who is] the Great Master Shixing of Mt. Baiyun. The Master's disciples had already organized the assembly accordingly. At the hour of the rat on the tenth day of the fourth moon of the forty-sixth year (of the sixty-year cycle; between 11 P.M. of May 10 and 1 A.M. of May 11, 949), the Master left this world.
>
> *Oh! The boat of compassion having been destroyed*
> *Samsara will not attain the shore of salvation.*
> *The Dharma mountain having crumbled*
> *What have flying and walking creatures left to rely upon?*

The Life of Master Yunmen

One thousand monks and lay people participated at the funeral ceremonies that took place fifteen days after Master Yunmen's death. In accordance with the master's instructions, his corpse was put as it was into the burial site inside the master's living quarters. The stone inscriptions state that fifteen days after his death he still looked as if he were alive. The biography of the *Record of Yunmen* contains additional details about the master's death and burial:

> On the tenth day of the fourth month of Qianhe 7, Master Yunmen passed away. In the morning he had composed a message to take leave from the sovereign and at the same time set forth his testament. Then he had folded his legs and died. Having had the honor of receiving an imperial gift of a stupa inscription, it was ordered in the Master's last will that his body was to be placed as it was inside his living quarters, and that the stupa inscription donated by the sovereign be properly displayed there. [He had ordered them] not to build a special stupa. In accordance with these instructions, the disciples buried the Master in his living quarters and considered his stupa to be there.

The sadness that prevailed at the funeral is described with the poetic license typical of Chinese inscriptions:

> On this day the drifting clouds stood [respectfully] still and the grave tree withered. The cry of the mountain's lone monkeys sharpened the pain of the loss, and invisible birds' voices that pierced the woods heightened the regret and sadness of separation. The mourners hid [their faces] in their collars and stood around crying.

The mummy of Master Yunmen (1928 photo)

The Mummy

If the participants at Yunmen's funeral had been stunned that the corpse of the master looked as if it were alive, they were soon to experience still greater wonders. The second stone inscription states that in the seventeenth year from Yunmen's death the master appeared to the magistrate Ruan Shaozhuang in a dream and instructed him to open his grave. When it was opened, the master's body was found unchanged except that its hair and finger- and toenails had grown longer. The eyes were half open and glistened like pearls, the teeth sparkled like snow, and a mystical glow filled the whole room. Several thousand monks and lay persons are said to have witnessed this.

By imperial edict the mummy of Yunmen was brought with great ceremony into Guangzhou, the capital, where it was honored for an entire month—even by the current ruler Liu Chang, who had more sympathy for Daoism. This last of the rulers of the Southern Han empire also bestowed a posthumous honorary title upon the master and gave the monastery at the foot of Mt. Yunmen the name it carries to this day: Chan Monastery of Great Awakening. The mummy was returned to the Yunmen monastery, where it remained for more than one thousand years. Having disappeared in the mid-1970s during the Cultural Revolution, it must at this point be considered lost.

The modern replica of the mummy (1990 photo)

The Teaching of Master Yunmen

■ ■ ■

Medicine for a Disease

A Chan text such as the *Record of Yunmen* is neither a philosophy textbook nor a systematic presentation of Chan thought or practice; rather, it is a collection consisting primarily of formal talks given by a master to practitioners, and of his conversations with them, and thus contains concrete examples of his teaching. It is practical rather than theoretical, pedagogic rather than philosophical. This overall characteristic can be seen in both the content and the form of this and similar texts: they contain formal talks and dialogues that thoroughly address the situation and needs of the specific group or individual to which they were directed, and as such they are medicine for a specific ill rather than metaphysical statements. Even their later arrangement into a succession of talks and dialogues[1] betrays the pedagogical intent, since the editors based their arrangement predominantly on particular ways of teaching rather than criteria of content. The title they affixed to the first sections of the *Record of Yunmen* makes the same point: "duiji" means "to correspond to the occasion" (or alternatively, "to correspond to individual abilities").

---

[1] See the short textual history in the Materials section at the end of this volume.

The outer circumstances are comparatively well known: these teachings were directed at monks (and some lay followers) who lived at a Chan monastery in China's deep south around the middle of the tenth century. Most listeners as well as the teacher had taken the monastic precepts, wore monk's robes, had left their families, and had few personal possessions besides bowl, staff, robe, and possibly some books. These monks stood in the long tradition of Buddhist monasticism that had begun centuries before the beginning of the common era and has today spread all over the globe. In spite of the originality of Chan pedagogy and the universal appeal of its teachings, one should never forget that their original setting was the traditional Chinese Buddhist monastery with its particular organization, rhythm, rules of conduct, and atmosphere. Many questions and answers relate to thoughts, scriptures, and practices of the Buddhist tradition, well known to the monks of that tradition but often obscure to us. Thus a good number of pronouncements are likely to be even more puzzling to us than they no doubt were to their original audience; similarly, many references that were obvious to them now need to be belabored in footnotes or escape us altogether. It is often difficult or impossible to judge what the original audience understood and in what ways that understanding differs from that of this translator and of you, the reader; thus the question of what should be understood (and explained) and what must be (or is better) left unexplained is indeed a difficult koan for the translator.

Matching Concepts

Translation must by its very nature employ concepts coming from different languages and cultures. When Buddhism was introduced to China, the monks and philosophers had to find Chinese counterparts to the foreign Indian concepts. The terms they came up with were predominantly of Daoist origin. Their effort was called "matching concepts" *(keyi)* and flourished in the third, fourth, and fifth centuries. In a broader sense, Chan as a whole can be regarded as a case of "matching concepts": though the Chan masters expressed themselves in ways that seem radically different from the Buddha's, one may hold with Edward Conze that they have come closer to the heart of the Buddha's message than anyone else.[1] But the Chan, Zen, and Son masters of present and past make an even greater claim: they insist over and over again that they are no different from the buddhas and the founders of Chan and that we, if we would only realize this, are the same, too. Thus, in spite of the various historical and cultural differences, the claim is made by the masters themselves that the essence of Chan, Zen, and Son teaching is the same throughout—and that it is identical to that of the Buddha's teaching. My introduction to Yunmen's teaching is an attempt to analyze this essence of Chan/Zen/Son teaching in modern terms and to illustrate it primarily with sayings of Yunmen.

When matching concepts, the importing culture must furnish new concepts. It usually draws them from its own philosophical and religious traditions. The ancient Chinese used Daoist terms, and we use terms stemming from our Western intellectual heritage. For example, D. T. Suzuki, the great Japanese pioneer who first presented Zen texts and doctrine to the West, made use of a variety of terms drawn from Western philosophy, psychology, and religion. A few decades later, it may seem easy to criticize such pioneering efforts. However, one must not forget that those able to criticize would never even have become informed about and interested in the matter had it

---

[1] Edward Conze, *A Short History of Buddhism* (London: George Allen & Unwin, 1980), p. 93.

not first been laid out in the very terms they now consider inadequate.

The fact that concepts can be matched, however inadequately, points to a sphere that transcends historical circumstance and linguistic barriers. This is the existential sphere in which, regardless of one's race, education, or nationality, one immediately recognizes humanity in the eye of the other. It is the sphere of *being a person,* regardless of time and place. And just this is the basic concern of Buddhism.

The Basic Problem

Tradition has it that the Buddha, faced with questions of a metaphysical nature, once used a parable to explain his view: such questions, he said, were like those of a person wounded by an arrow who would like to know what the arrow consisted of, where it came from, etc., rather than seek to have it removed and the wound healed. His teaching, he said, was designed to heal, not to answer such questions. This illness, one might add, is a universal one, afflicting all persons alike.

Buddhism is thus an art of healing rather than a philosophy, an aid to help one towards salvation rather than a philosophical edifice. The Zen teacher tries to get his students to take care of their problem, and he steers them towards that goal by whatever means he sees fit, just like that father in the *Lotus Sutra* who had to resort to various tricks in order to save his children who were obliviously playing in a burning house. This is the kind of teaching that we encounter in the present translation.

But in the course of Buddhism's history and its journey through various countries and cultures, many rituals, much imagery, a good deal of magic, and also many philosophical movements developed and flourished within it. A large part of the baggage that accumulated on the journey through India, Central

Asia, and China was gradually thrown away in Chan. At Chan's inception we already detect the will to get back to the essentials and concentrate on the one thing that ultimately matters in Buddhism: the removal of the arrow, the realization that turned Gautama into the Buddha—awakening (satori).

Chan texts are impressive documents of this endeavor and orientation: practitioners ask their teacher about what occupies them in their striving towards awakening and is central to their life and practice, and the teacher by his presence and teaching points towards the very same thing. The content and methods of teaching are as strictly adapted to the particular circumstances and audience as a medicine to the illness it must remove. Yet, regardless of time, place, and circumstance, the goal remains the same thing: healing and recovery. But healing and recovery from what?

Ancient Buddhist scriptures contain various analyses of the core problem that drove the Buddha on his quest and is the raison d'être of his teaching. Best known is the explanation that the Buddha is said to have given in the first speech after his awakening. In this speech he presented the Four Noble Truths, the first two of which consist of the Buddha's diagnosis of the basic problem lying at the core of human existence:

> This, O monks, is the noble truth of suffering: birth is suffering, old age is suffering, disease is suffering, death is suffering, union with what one dislikes is suffering, separation from what one likes is suffering, not obtaining one's wish is suffering, in brief, the five kinds of objects of attachment are suffering.

> This, O monks, is the noble truth of the origin of suffering: it is the thirst which leads from rebirth to rebirth, accompanied by pleasure and covetousness, which finds its plea-

sure here and there: the thirst for pleasure, the thirst for existence, the thirst for impermanence.[1]

This explanation (very concise by Indian standards) is by Chan teachers once more distilled and expressed in many concrete and original ways. To take just one formulation that stems from Master Yunmen:

> The monk inquired, "What's the problem?"
> The Master said, "You don't notice the stench of your own shit!"[2]

The directness of the question and the unerring aim and uncouth terseness of the reply are characteristic of Chan as a whole. The Japanese Zen master Bankei (1622–1693) said the same in a more civilized manner:

> Your self-partiality is at the root of all your illusions. There aren't any illusions when you don't have this preference for yourself.[3]

Yunmen and numerous other masters observed that "what one does not see at all is one's own eye." This statement points in the same direction: the "I" that always stands at the center of the world and ultimately sees and judges everything and everybody from this perspective; just this "I" that desires and rejects, thirsts for love, power, and fulfillment, and experiences frustration and pain, wants to live and yet must die, seeks to preserve itself and puts everything in motion to this end, *is* itself yet has to

---

[1] Étienne Lamotte, *History of Indian Buddhism* (Louvain, Belgium: Peeters Press, 1988), p. 26.

[2] See section 271.

[3] Norman Waddell, *The Unborn: The Life and Teaching of Zen Master Bankei* (San Francisco: North Point Press, 1984), p. 49.

search for itself. This "I" is here at stake. We have already seen that, when Yunmen went to face Master Muzhou, he expressed just this:

> Muzhou asked, "What are you here for?"
>
> Yunmen said, "I am not yet clear about myself."
> (Section 278)

Whether one likes it or not, it is inevitable that just one's "I," the one around whose weal and woe the whole world turns, is the central affair of each person. That one has no clarity about one's "I" is more than simple ignorance, which would not be a problem: the proverb says, "What the eye does not see, the heart cannot grieve over." Rather, this ignorance is born from reflection; that is, it is a *knowing* ignorance.

> Once Master Yunmen asked, "What's wrong with some-one who is in the dark about himself?"
>
> He answered on behalf of the silent monks, "That ought not to be a problem for a great man!" (Section 251)

This kind of ignorance is found only in human beings and goes together with the knowledge that one has to die as well as the concern about illness and old age that, according to legend, were the motives driving the young Gautama on his quest for ultimate liberation. This ignorance is rooted in the "I" that, as the seeing agent, stands in the center as the subject and simultaneously can and must make itself its own object. The human being, in contrast to plants or animals, not only has objects and finds itself among them, it simultaneously is its own object. Conscious of itself and also able to see itself as the object of another person, it can have a sense of shame and be embarrassed. Thus the Dutch anthropologist F. Buytendjik rightly said that anthropology is found in its entirety in man's dress. The human being can point to itself and say "this is me," yet the pointing person escapes its own grasp and must ask: "Who am I?" The human being thus rests in itself, yet is lost inside and outside; senses itself intimately, yet remains a dark hole; is itself, yet must first truly become itself. This mode of being has been well described by the late German philosopher and anthropologist Helmuth Plessner, who called it "ex-centric" in contrast to the centric mode of being of animals, who rest in themselves.[1] The being with this particular inner rift is inevitably not at ease with itself; it is driven, frustrated, concerned about itself. Seeking its own center and peace of mind, it chases after happiness and rest, and finds itself able neither to arrive at this goal nor to abandon the search for it.

When a human being observes itself or its own thoughts, it finds that there is always an observer and something observed. The observer as such is forever unobserved; he or she always stands at the center and looks. He or she is in one way like someone in a watchtower: whatever this observer chooses to throw light on it sees, but it itself cannot but stay in the dark. Yet, unlike a watchtower man, the self-conscious human observer can recede, put itself into another watchtower and throw light on the first one, and then into one more and so on—but the observer occupying the new watchtower always remains invisible, a black hole forever unable to grasp itself *as subject*. It is this state of affairs, I think, that the young Yunmen pointed to when he told Master Muzhou that he had no clarity about himself.

But this ever receding subject must not be mistaken for the goal of Chan and Buddhism; rather, it is the starting point, defined in the first Noble Truth with utmost simplicity as "suffer-

---

[1] English translations of the major works of this important thinker appear to be lacking as yet. The concept of ex-centricity is developed in his major work, *Die Stufen des Organischen und der Mensch* (The Stages of the Organic and Man), which was completed in 1926, almost simultaneously with Heidegger's *Sein und Zeit* (Being and Time).

ing." Yunmen's search for the objectifying and objectified "I" is thus immediately and decisively rejected by Master Muzhou: "Useless stuff!" What Yunmen awakened to at that moment, and what forms the basis of his teacher Muzhou's comment, is not this subject but rather the True Self. In the Chan tradition it is often compared to a light that illumines all objects. Yunmen says the following about this light:

> Every person originally has the radiant light—yet when it is looked at, it is not seen: dark and obscure! (Section 143)

Though clearly apparent to the awakened master, this self must remain "dark and hidden" to the self-centered "I":

> If you want to freely live or die, go or stay, to take off or put on [your clothes], then right now recognize the man who is listening to my discourse. He is without form, without characteristics, without root, without source, and without any dwelling place, yet he is brisk and lively. As for all his manifold responsive activities, the place where they are carried on is, in fact, no-place. Therefore, when you look for him, he retreats farther and farther; when you seek him, he turns more and more the other way: this is called the "Mystery."[1]

Duality

The most basic problem of the human being consists in its particular structure as a subject-object being. As soon as we speak of an "I" that is distinct from any "other," we speak of an "I" that has the unique capacity of reflecting upon itself and thus is both subject and object. In the Buddhist tradition, this state of affairs is

---

[1] *Record of Linji,* T47: 498c8–11 (Sasaki translation, p. 15).

expressed by the term *duality*. It manifests itself not only in the knowing ignorance of young Yunmen ("I am not clear about myself"), but also in the separation of the seeing, hearing, desiring "I" from the objects of its seeing, hearing, and desire: the central "I" cannot but see everything from its own position— and just because of this it can never see things the way they are, but forever only the way it sees them. This inescapable condition is beautifully described in a story by the Chinese sage Zhuangzi (Chuangtzu):[1]

> In the bald and barren north, there is a dark sea, the Lake of Heaven. In it is a fish which is several thousand miles across, and no one knows how long. His name is Kun. There is also a bird there, named Peng, with a back like Mount Tai and wings like clouds filling the sky. He beats the whirlwind, leaps into the air, and rises up ninety thousand miles, cutting through clouds and mist, shouldering the blue sky, and then he turns his eyes south and prepares to journey to the southern darkness.
>
> The little quail laughs at him, saying, "Where does he think *he's* going? I give a great leap and fly up, but I never get more than ten or twelve yards before I come down fluttering among the weeds and brambles. And that's the best kind of flying anyway! Where does he think *he's* going?"

This story by Zhuangzi illustrates that in general people do not see objects "objectively," with a cool observing eye; instead, the seer, caught up in his own position and intent on his own profit, immediately and inevitably sees and judges phenomena "subjectively," from its particular point of view. The "I" at the center of the world, simultaneously holding on to and having

---

[1] This story is found at the beginning of Zhuangzi's chapter 1.

absolutely no hold of itself, also wants more than anything else itself and its own advantage; yet it does not have the slightest clue what that ultimately is. In pursuit of it, it drives on and on, never able to make the fleeting moment of satisfaction eternal and yet unable to stop trying.[1] This is what is called "thirst" in the Buddha's second Noble Truth—and the seeing yet blind "I" at its origin is the ultimate reason that one sees the mote in the eye of the other but not the beam in one's own and that one has the natural tendency to hate the stench of others but not necessarily one's own.

Because of that clinging to itself and to its objects and the simultaneous deep separation both from itself, all others, and other things, the human being is profoundly unfree and dissatisfied. Driven by the bond to itself and its objects, it is without respite forced to judge and to desire or to reject. It is full of itself and of countless things, thoughts, plans, and desires. The restless chaos that fills its heart and head, well described by James Joyce in *Ulysses,* is familiar to those who try to concentrate on something, be it a piece of music, a thought, or a koan.

Seeking to overcome this inner and outer rift and alienation that is called "duality," the human being not only gets attached to objects of a profane nature; lofty teachings, such as those of Buddhism, and even the Buddha himself, are objects, too. Yunmen says:

> As long as the light has not yet broken through, there are two kinds of disease: 1. The first consists in seeing oneself facing objects and being left in the dark about everything. 2. The second consists in having been able to pierce through to the emptiness of all separate entities (dhar-

---

[1] As is to be expected with something so profoundly human, there are many expressions of this state to be found in the arts, from Goethe's *Faust* (part I) to the Rolling Stones' "I Can't Get No Satisfaction."

mas)—yet there still is something that in a hidden way is like an object.

[Views about] the body of the teaching also exhibit two kinds of disease: 1. Having been able to reach the body of the Buddhist teaching, one still has subjective views and is at the margin of that teaching because one has not gotten rid of one's attachment to it. 2. Even though one has managed to penetrate through to the body of the Buddhist teaching, one is still unable to let go of it. But if one examines this [teaching] thoroughly, it's stone-dead. That's also a disease! (Section 193)

The overcoming of the disease of duality, the letting go of all subject-object-hood, including oneself and the Buddhist teaching, is the liberation from all attachment of which Yunmen and other Buddhist teachers speak. It is an absolute and limitless emptying. This liberation was expressed in the third Noble Truth:

> This, O monks, is the noble truth of the cessation of suffering: the extinction of that thirst by means of the complete annihilation of desire, by banishing desire, by renouncing it, by being delivered from it, by leaving it no place.[1]

Again, Master Yunmen found simple words to express this: "My brothers, if there is one who has attained it, he passes his days in conformity with the ordinary" (section 46). What a contrast to the restless drive for the extraordinary that has cast its spell on man! The essence of this being-at-home is pointed out in the last line of the quatrain cited in the Introduction:

> *[Chan] is transmitted outside of established doctrine;*
> *it does not institute words. [Rather,]*

---

[1] Lamotte, *History of Indian Buddhism,* p. 26.

The Teaching of Master Yunmen

It points directly to the human being's heart:
whoever sees his own nature becomes an awakened buddha.

This indicates the solution of the problem that beset the young Yunmen when he went to see Master Muzhou. It found another expression in the *Inscription on Trusting in Mind*, which Yunmen cited. There the essence of buddhahood is described in terms of not-twoness or non-duality:

The realm of non-thinking
can hardly be fathomed by cognition;
in the sphere of genuine suchness
there is neither "I" nor "other."[1]

But let us for the time being keep to questions rather than answers; after all, Yunmen does not tire of stressing their importance:

Someone asked, "What is the fundamental teaching?"
Master Yunmen said, "No question, no answer."
(Section 30)

What Can One Do?

It is striking how little concrete and practical advice one finds in Yunmen's instructions (and, for that matter, in most classical Chan texts). Instead of telling his disciples what they should do, how they should meditate, etc., he keeps asking them the same questions: What is your problem? Why are you a monk? Why are you here? What is there to learn here? What is it that you ought to realize?

So let me ask you all: What has so far been the matter with you? What do you lack? If I tell you that nothing whatso-

---

[1] T51: 457b17–18; see also section 27.

ever is the matter I've already buried you; you yourself must arrive at that realization! (Section 7)

Whether you are an innocent beginner or seasoned adept, you must show some spirit! Don't vainly memorize [other people's] sayings: a little bit of reality is better than a lot of illusion. [Otherwise,] you'll just go on deceiving yourself.

What is the matter with you? Come forward [and tell me]! (Section 61)

Again and again the Master urges his disciples to find out what bothers them and to do this on their own, without blindly relying on anything or anyone, including teachers or holy scriptures. In a nutshell, his central piece of advice is: "Find out what's wrong, and it will all come together" (Section 67).

This advice is similar to that given by Bodhidharma to Huike, who was later to become the second patriarch of Chan: "Show me your heart-mind, and I will pacify it!" According to legend, Huike had cut off one arm as a desperate proof of his determination to receive the teaching of Bodhidharma, whereupon the following dialogue is said to have occurred:

Huike: "Please, Master, bring peace into my heart-mind!"

Bodhidharma: "Show me your heart-mind, and I will pacify it."

Huike: "I have searched for it, but I could not find it."

Bodhidharma: "If you could search for it, how could it be your very own heart-mind? And how should I bring peace to it?"[1]

In Chan literature there are countless examples of a similar kind: "Who is it that is asking me?" or "Who is listening to my words

---

[1] *Collection from the Founder's Halls,* 1.73, 6–9.

The Teaching of Master Yunmen

"What is it?" penned by Shin'ichi Hisamatsu

right now?" or simply "What is it?"[1] One's own true heart, the seeker's true self: just this appears to be that "very own matter of yours which does not allow anybody to step in for you":[2]

> Someone asked Master Yunmen, "What is most urgent for me?"
>
> The Master said, "The very *you* who is afraid that he doesn't know!" (Section 38)

Again and again, the master urges his disciples to find out where the problem lies:

---

[1] The latter is one of the most frequently used koans in Korean Zen. When I asked the head monk of the new monastery at Mt. Yunmen whether he exclusively recited Amida Buddha's name or whether he also practiced with koans, he said he was struggling with a variation of this: "Who is it that recites Amida Buddha's name?"

[2] See section 46.

Someone asked, "Life-and-death is here; how am I to cope with it?"

The Master said, "Where is it?" (Section 51)

But Yunmen does not simply throw questions back at the questioners; rather, he uses any and all means at his disposal to drive the students to deal with their problem. In conjunction with this, he repeatedly and insistently warns them to rely on no one and nothing:

> You must neither fall for the tricks of others nor simply accept their directives. The instant you see an old monk open his mouth, you tend to stuff those big rocks right into yours, and when you cluster in little groups to discuss [his words], you're exactly like those green flies on shit that struggle back to back to gobble it up! What a shame, brothers! (Section 41)

Whatever prop one makes use of—pilgrimages, holy scriptures, lofty teachings, a meditation method, a master, the teaching of Yunmen—Yunmen does not spare anything. The moment he discovers that one is relying on something or someone, he strikes with his staff or his sharp tongue. Other Chan masters are very similar in this respect:

> The old masters couldn't help it. When they saw you run about aimlessly, they said to you "supreme wisdom (bodhi) and nirvana." They really buried you; they drove in a stake and tied you to it.[1] Again, when they saw that you didn't understand, they said to you: "It's not bodhi and nirvana." Knowing this sort of thing already shows that you're down on your luck; [but to make matters

---

[1] See *Record of Linji* (T47: 497c11): "Bodhi and nirvana are like hitching posts for asses."

worse,] you're looking for comments and explanations by others. You exterminators of Buddhism, you've been like this all along! And where has this brought you today? (Section 144)

Though the teaching methods of these masters show many variations, they nevertheless have a common purpose: to make the seeker come to himself and to get rid of anything that is a hindrance in that respect. The shouts and beatings, the sarcastic remarks and ironic gestures, the acerbic criticism and verbal attacks rife in this and other Chan texts are neither an end in themselves nor nonsensical; they are designed to remove all props, to take away everything on which one could possibly rely, in order to throw the seeker back upon himself and let him come to himself.

The classical masters hardly provide the kind of detailed guidance about breath, meditation posture, and other concrete aspects of religious practice that modern disciples have come to demand and that some masters furnish. It is of course possible that they or the editors thought it unnecessary to mention such matters, since they were so obvious and common in monastic communities; but it could also be a significant omission that has to be seen in this context of "removing props." One notices the latter in many Chan stories, for instance the following famous one:

When at Demboin, Baso used to sit cross-legged all day and meditating. His master, Nangaku Yejo (Nan-yueh Huai-jang, 677–744), saw him and asked:

"What seekest thou here thus sitting cross-legged?"

"My desire is to become a Buddha."

Thereupon the master took up a piece of brick and began to polish it hard on the stone near by.

"What workest thou on so, my master?" asked Baso.

"I am trying to turn this into a mirror."

"No amount of polishing will make a mirror of the brick, sir."

"If so, no amount of sitting cross-legged as thou doest will make of thee a Buddha," said the master.

"What shall I have to do then?"

"It is like driving a cart; when it moveth not, wilt thou whip the cart or the ox?"

Baso made no answer.

The master continued: "Wilt thou practice this sitting cross-legged in order to attain dhyāna[1] or to attain Buddhahood? If it is dhyāna, dhyāna does not consist in sitting or lying; if it is Buddhahood, the Buddha has no fixed forms. As he has no abiding place anywhere, no one can take hold of him, nor can he be let go. If thou seekest Buddhahood by thus sitting cross-legged, thou murderest him. So long as thou freest thyself not from sitting so, thou never comest to the truth."[2]

As far as we can tell by looking at all transmitted sources, Master Yunmen was consistent and radical in his attack on any kind of prop. If someone relies on him as his teacher, he shrugs it off ("I can do nothing but eat, shit, and piss!"); if someone relies on meditation, he criticizes him ("this is just something you could learn on the meditation bench"); if someone trusts in Buddha, he calls the Buddha an old Indian fellow who is long dead; and if someone relies on Buddhist teaching, he does not hesitate to remove that prop, too ("that's nothing but dream talk"). This attack on any kind of prop does not stop at any

---

[1] Total meditative concentration; the pronunciation of this Sanskrit term was imitated by the Chinese as "Chan," the term used by early Chinese Buddhists for meditation and later also for the Chan (Zen) school.

[2] The translation (but not the note on dhyāna) is by D. T. Suzuki, *Essays in Zen Buddhism, First Series* (New York: Harper & Brothers, 1949), p. 234.

point. The master's teaching, the Chan patriarchs, the sutras, thinking, not-thinking, seeking, questioning—*any* kind of prop suffers the same fate. All methods, ways, or devices—i.e., anything that mediates—is swept away in order to let the most immediate reveal itself.

The Pathless Path

But what remains if all paths, all ways, and all props are pulled away? Isn't that a hopeless situation with no way out? This dilemma and the Chan way to its resolution are delineated in a conversation that took place around the middle of this century between the modern Japanese Zen teacher Shin'ichi Hisamatsu[1] and the American professor and seeker Bernard Phillips:

> Phillips: "If you follow any way, you will never get there; and if you do not follow any way, you will never get there. So one faces a dilemma."
>
> Hisamatsu: "Let that dilemma be your way! (I.e., it is that very dilemma that is the way you must follow!)"[2]

A very similar statement closes an anecdote handed down from the eighth century. In this context, Master Shitou's answer characterizes the whole of Southern Chan (which is the only kind that survived):

> When Chan Master Yaoshan Weiyan first visited Shitou,[3] he asked: "I have a superficial knowledge of the three

---

[1] See Steven Antinoff, "The Problem of the Human Person and the Resolution to That Problem in the Religio-Philosophical Thought of the Zen Master Shin'ichi Hisamatsu" (Ph.D. diss., Temple University, 1990).

[2] Richard DeMartino, "The Zen Understanding of Man" (Ph.D. diss., Temple University, 1969), p. 274.

[3] Shitou Xiqian (700–790).

[Buddhist] vehicles' twelve divisions of teachings. Now I keep hearing of Southern [Chan's characterization as] 'directly pointing to man's heart.' This is something I really haven't yet understood, and I humbly request your compassionate instruction."

Shitou said: "This way will not do, and any other way will not do either. No way, neither this way nor any other way will do. What do you do?"[1]

Because of his inner rift and alienation, man is forced to find ways to inner peace and contentment. Neither his diverse roles in society nor wealth nor the various kinds of therapy, etc., are ultimately capable of bringing about this peace; they may be able to lead to or mediate *something,* but not that which is immediate par excellence and thus is exactly *not something.*[2] In the words of the Chan masters: "What you find outside is not the treasure of your own home."

This does not mean, however, that one can simply abandon seeking. One cannot help but seek this ultimate contentment, even if one realizes that it is not something that can be found in this way. This is the point made by Professor Phillips, who had traversed the world in search of a path, and it is congruent with Master Shitou's statement. The closing remarks of Hisamatsu and Shitou have an identical thrust: they point out the Zen way by challenging one to take this very dilemma as the way. In other words, it is exactly the no-way-out situation in which the human being finds itself—the fundamental and unbridgeable inner cleavage of that being which is conscious of itself—that is said to be the way. We will see later that in Zen the

---

[1] *Record of Mazu,* ZZ119: 408c14–17.

[2] For the different meanings of "nothingness" in this context see Shin'ichi Hisamatsu, "The Characteristics of Oriental Nothingness," *Philosophical Studies of Japan 2* (1960), pp. 65–97.

ultimate actualization of this pathless path is called "great doubt."

> Someone asked Yunmen, "Though this is constantly my most pressing concern, I cannot find any way in. Please, Master, show me a way in!"
> The Master said, "Just in your present concern there is a way." (Section 87)

In other words, just in the inability to find an access there is a way. In countless talks of masters this dilemma is brought home to the audience in the form of a challenge. The following episode has been transmitted about Yunmen:

> As a monk stood waiting, Master Yunmen said to him: "I want neither words nor no words. What do you say?"[1]

Hisamatsu put this into a more general form: *"Dōshitemo ikanakereba dō suru ka?":* "Nothing will do. What do you do?" He called this the "fundamental koan"—i.e., the koan that is the common denominator of the thousands of extant koans.

Koan

What is a koan? Among the many current definitions and descriptions, that of Richard DeMartino stands out as both the shortest and the most precise: "A koan is a Zen presentation in the form of a Zen challenge."[2] The word "koan" was in Yunmen's time still predominantly used as a juridical term (a case)[3]

---

[1] *Record of Yunmen,* T47: 572b20–21.

[2] Richard DeMartino, "On Zen Communication," *Communication 8,* no. 1 (1983).

[3] See section 46, p. 107, note 4.

and only later acquired its present meaning. Other terms, such as *yinyuan* (event) or *ze* (case), were employed to describe Zen presentations that had the form of a Zen challenge. Such presentations were often short stories of sometimes legendary character that were told and retold in Chan circles and were also used as Zen challenges by masters to their audience.

In the late ninth and tenth centuries a development set in that was to have a deep influence on Zen up to this day. Some of the stories of encounters between masters and their colleagues or masters and disciples were applied more and more consciously as a means of Zen teaching and training. By the eleventh century we find whole collections of such stories (koan collections), which were commented upon by masters in poetic or prose form and much used by students and teachers alike.

It is around this time and in these circumstances that the word *koan* became popular. With the great master Dahui (1089–1163) and his explicit instructions for koan training,[1] the use of koans in Zen teaching and practice reached a first peak. A second and third can be seen in the widespread use of koans that developed in Korea and Japan (in the latter case, particularly through the influence of the masters Daitō and Hakuin, and the latter's disciple Tōrei). The use of koans has since become even more systematic and can today be observed in Zen circles all over the globe.[2]

The early phase of the frequent use of such stories in Zen teaching and training is marked by a figure of central importance: our Master Yunmen. Though he did not yet call them "koans," we have hundreds of examples of his explicit use of

---

[1] See, for instance, his letters, some of which were translated by Christopher Cleary in *Swampland Flowers: The Letters and Lectures of Zen Master Ta Hui* (New York: Grove Press, 1977).

[2] See also the Ways of Teachings section on p. 70.

such stories or quotes as a Zen challenge. This makes him a pioneer of koan use. In particular, the second fascicle of the *Record of Yunmen*[1] is full of examples where the master cites a saying or tells an anecdote and uses that as a challenge to his audience.

> Master Yunmen cited the words of Master Liangsui: "What everybody knows, I know it all; but nobody knows what I know."
>
> Master Yunmen asked his audience, "What is it that Liangsui knows?"[2]

On another occasion, he challenged a monk:

> Master Yunmen mentioned the following story:
> A monk asked Xuefeng for instruction. Xuefeng said to him: "What is it?" At these words the monk attained great awakening.
>
> Master Yunmen said: "What is it that Xuefeng had told him?" (Section 154)

Passages from Buddhist scriptures are used as koans in similar ways (e.g., sections 173, 195). Inevitably, such stories and questions are difficult to understand; as presentations of Zen they are expressions of non-duality, and in their function as a Zen challenge they should assist the practitioner in breaking through the confines of dualistic understanding. Seen from the standpoint of ordinary dualistic logic, such statements often break all rules and make no sense whatsoever. However, this is not so by chance; these often paradoxical expressions of non-duality make sense in their own way:

> The ultimate objective [of Chan] remains the same: to know and appreciate who one is beyond "the fold of rea-

---

[1] See section 145 ff.

[2] T47: 557c13–15.

son," that is, beyond the [dualistic] subject-object structure of intellection. Toward this end the koan, a kind of question, problem, challenge, or demand presented by and upon the initiative of the master, is intended to serve a twofold function. The first is to penetrate to the depths and quicken at its source the deeply buried or deceptively concealed basic underlying concern of the ego in ego-consciousness. The second is, while stirring this fundamental longing and its quest, to keep them properly rooted and directed. For it is not sufficient that they simply be aroused. They must, in order to avoid the many deceptive and delusive pitfalls in which they may become attenuated or go astray, also be carefully guided and even fostered.[1]

The function of the Zen master in general and of his special methods of instruction (for instance, the koans) becomes clearer when seen from this perspective. Many talks and dialogues that came to be used as koans show the human situation in highly concentrated form, and seek to bring this to a point of coagulation in the practitioner, fan the fire of seeking and doubt, and simultaneously keep the seeker from getting sidetracked. And since everything that is an object—including all objects of thought, all Zen teachings, and whatever people say—is a sidetrack, Yunmen says:

> If in my assembly someone's ability is manifested in a phrase, you'll ponder in vain. Even if, in order to make progress, you sorted out all Chan teachings with their thousand differences and myriad distinctions, your mistake would still consist in searching for proclamations from other people's tongues. (Section 1)

---

[1] DeMartino, "The Human Situation and Zen Buddhism," p. 156.

But if the aim is not an object, what is it? It is exactly the nothing that is beyond any objectification: the "master in your own house," the one who sees and hears and reads:

> In the meantime, you cheat the master in your own house. Is that all right? When you manage to find a little slime on my ass, you lick it off, take it to be your own self, and say: "I understand Chan, I understand the Dao!" Even if you manage to read the whole Buddhist canon—so what?! (Section 144)

This master in one's own house, one's True Self, is no object; and as long as objects are sought, nothing but objects will be found. But since no search can be without an object, all searching is ultimately a chase after a phantom:

> Haven't you read the *Shūrangama Sutra,* which says, "Sentient beings are all upside down; they delude themselves and chase after things." (Section 195)

Yunmen then adds, "If they could handle things, they would be identical to the Buddha."

Letting Go

The breakthrough that is often called "awakening," "enlightenment," or "satori" consists in the thorough overcoming of man's structural duality. This overcoming has been expressed by many terms, such as "awakening to oneself," "letting go," and "seeing one's own nature." Their common denominator is the overcoming of man's inner rift or duality, which manifests itself in inner and outer attachment and alienation. Buddhism aims at the removal of this shackle. Buddhist scriptures do not seem to tire of explaining non-duality and its various manifestations. For instance, one of the most popular Buddhist scriptures in China, the *Vimalakîrti Sutra* (which was and is much read in Zen circles), explains:

> Enlightened wisdom is non-duality, since there is neither mind (manas) nor object (dharma).[1]

However, this does not mean that there is no mind and therefore no subject anymore; rather, it points to the "true" or "selfless" or "formless" I or self—i.e., the self that is beyond any delimitations and opposition. None other than this self is called "Non-I" (anâtman) in Buddhism:

> To know that I (ātman) and Non-I (anātman) are no duality (advaya): this is the meaning of the term Non-I (anātman).[2]

Such a breakthrough is beyond the range of possibilities of the dualistic "I," which cannot but be attached to itself. Any method or way must originate in and serve such a self-attached "I"—whose dilemma consists in wanting to be at ease and at peace, yet being unable to achieve this. A living contradiction, the "I" must want itself yet longs to lose itself. It is caught in a vicious circle with no way out.

True *Gelassenheit*,[3] on the other hand, presupposes the I's letting go of itself—and it is just this letting go that Zen masters and their koans demand:

---

[1] Étienne Lamotte, *L'Enseignement de Vimalakīrti* (Louvain, Belgium: Institut Orientaliste, 1962), p. 195. Much of this scripture is devoted to a discussion of non-duality.

[2] Ibid., p. 166.

[3] This German term, much used by Meister Eckehart and other medieval German mystics and again by Heidegger and Heideggerians, signifies "composure" or "calmness" or "detachment." There seems to be no English equivalent which contains, as the German does, the root of "to let" or "to let go" *(lassen)*.

The Teaching of Master Yunmen

Master Xiangyan said: "It's like a man up in a tree, hanging from a branch by his mouth. His hands and feet cannot touch any branch, and his feet will not reach the trunk. Someone under the tree asks him what Bodhidharma intended when coming from the West. If he doesn't answer, he does not live up to the challenge. If he answers, he loses himself and his life. What should he do in this situation?"[1]

The vocabulary used in Zen for the breakthrough (letting go, great death, great birth, etc.) points to the fact that this is a radical and structural transformation of being human, not just a partial or relative one. Man's most fundamental attachment and at the same time his innermost rift and alienation must be fundamentally overcome. The *Record of Mazu* says:

Baizhang[2] asked Master Mazu[3], "What is essential in Buddhism?" Mazu replied, "Just that you let go of yourself and your life."[4]

The *Record of Yunmen* contains a similar statement. After having said that the twenty-eight Indian and six Chinese Patriarchs and all teachers under heaven are on the tip of his staff, Yunmen added:

But even if you'd manage to understand and discern this quite clearly, you'd still be but halfway there. As long as you don't let go, you're nothing but a wild fox ghost! (Section 146)

---

[1] *Gateless Barrier* (Ch. Wumenguan, Jap. Mumonkan), case 5 (T48: 293c1–4).

[2] Baizhang Huaihai (Jap. Hyakujō Ekai; 749–814).

[3] Mazu Daoyi (Jap. Baso Dōitsu; 709–788).

[4] *Record of Mazu*, ZZ119: 407a13.

Doubt

Koans and similar devices of the Zen teachers aim at providing help in letting go, and doubt plays a crucial role. In the Zen tradition one speaks of three major forces needed to drive the practitioner on: great trust, great effort, and great doubt. Every practitioner needs a good measure of trust in Buddhist teaching and in his teachers to even embark on this path. But in order to let go of oneself and everything else, one needs not only great trust but also a great effort. But the "I" that cannot know itself can by the same token also not let go of itself, because it is precisely its attachment to itself that makes it what it is. At the same time, it cannot stand holding on to itself and would like nothing better than to forget itself. The function of doubt lies precisely in the actualization of this double bind. While there is doubt involved when a student hears someone speak about Buddhist teaching or comes to see a teacher, he still holds on to whatever he can cling to and does not fully realize his existential impasse. The koans and other methods of instruction applied by Zen masters aim at its full realization and breakthrough.

> The preliminary objective of the koan is, therefore, to impel and incite not merely noetically, but affectively and physically as well, what in the terminology of Zen Buddhism is called the "great doubt"—and to do so in such a way that the ego becomes totally and existentially the "great doubt block" itself. Unless the ego does come to be the "great doubt block" itself, it can not be said to have arrived at the "great doubt."[1]

The master removes rigorously and systematically any means, any thing that the practitioner might hold on to. In this way, the

---

[1] DeMartino, "The Human Situation and Zen Buddhism," p. 159.

totally naked "I" with its basic rift and in its total impasse is crystallized and brought to a point. When Yunmen says "Find out what's wrong, and it will be all right" he aims just at this:

> The "great doubt" or "great doubt block" is no other than the intrinsic predicament of the ego in ego-consciousness totally and exhaustively exacerbated. The initial purpose of the koan—and the accompanying methodology of zazen, the sesshin, and sanzen—is to get the ego to arouse, crystallize, to bring entirely to the fore, and then, rather than endure, to become wholly and authentically the living contradiction which, as ego, it veritably is.[1]

Thus the "I" is itself the koan and realizes what is ultimately wrong: nothing it is or is not, nothing it has or has not, and nothing it does and nothing it refrains from doing will do (Hisamatsu: "Nothing will do"). Yet it is ceaselessly challenged to do something ("What do you do?"), to go on, let go, break through the impasse:

> Master Shishuang said, "How can you go on when you're on top of a one-hundred-foot pole?"[2]

Breakthrough

The goal of Buddhism is the breakthrough, the cutting of the root of all attachment and suffering, the death of the clinging "I" and thus of all desire. This "Great Death," this breakthrough to the most immediate and all-encompassing that is the True Self, is often compared to the awakening from deep sleep or the crack of dawn after a dark night of the soul. The "I" that was full of

---

[1] Ibid., p. 164.

[2] *Gateless Barrier* (Mumonkan), case 46 (T48: 298c12).

itself and desire and attachment yet tried to forget itself—the "I" that was immersed in life and death and was unable to cope satisfactorily with either, this "I" dies. Indeed, its "Great Death" is the breakthrough to the True Self: the "Great Birth." This is the awakening to the unfettered and formless self that is "at ease in the ordinary," happy and content with what it is and is not, has and has not. Master Yunmen sees nothing other than this self in any one of his disciples:

> In reality, there is not the slightest thing that could be the source of understanding or doubt for you. Rather, you have the one thing that matters, each and every one of you! Its great function manifests without the slightest effort on your part; you are no different from the patriarch-buddhas! (Section 41)

This self is the "man without rank" of which Linji (Rinzai) speaks,[1] and one's "true face," which is mentioned over and over again in Zen literature. It is bound to neither duality nor its negation and is free, content, and at ease under any circumstances.

> If you don't see any awakened ones (buddhas) above and sentient beings below, no mountain and river and world outside of you and no seeing, hearing, feeling, and knowing within: then you are like one who has died the great death and lives.[2]

It is for this reason that many Chan masters, including Yunmen, compare Chan teaching with a sword that both takes

---

[1] *Record of Linji,* T47: 496c10 (Sasaki translation, p. 3).

[2] *Blue Cliff Record,* case 6, T48: 146c8–10.

and gives life:[1] it kills the clinging and suffering "I" and is the midwife for the birth of the limitless, selfless, compassionate self that is no-thing and everything. The masters can be a guide towards this exactly because they have themselves gone through it. In the words of Master Yuanwu Keqin (1063–1135):

> If Yunmen were not a man who has broken through with his whole being and attained great freedom, how could he die with you and be born with you? Why can he? Because he is free from the numerous [dualistic] leaking points such as "gain" and "loss," "is" and "is not."[2]

Non-Duality

For this selfless self there is, if one puts it negatively, "neither mind nor objects."[3] Yunmen states similarly that "in the sphere of genuine suchness there is neither 'I' nor 'other.' "[4] Such statements express the core of Buddhist teaching, namely, not-twoness or non-duality. Countless texts and passages of the Buddhist tradition explain this concept. The *Vimalakīrti Sutra*,[5] whose entirety turns around non-duality, says for instance:

> To enter non-duality means to see that "I" and "not-I" are not two.

Master Yunmen often expresses the same in more concrete terms: "The lantern is your self" (section 150), or "the whole

---

[1] See the note to section 24, p. 96.

[2] *Blue Cliff Record,* case 15, T48: 155c3–5.

[3] Lamotte, *L'Enseignement de Vimalakīrti,* p. 195.

[4] See section 27 and its note.

[5] Lamotte, *L'Enseignement de Vimalakīrti,* p. 308.

world is you" (section 195). But one must not fail to point out that this nonduality is not equal to a simple oneness that again stands opposite plurality or duality. Thus Yunmen criticizes a monk:

> Yunmen asked a monk, "An old man said, 'In the realm of nondualism there is not the slightest obstacle between self and other.' What about Japan and Korea in this context?"
> The monk said, "They are not different."
> The Master remarked, "You go to hell." (Sect. 272)

Genuine non-duality cannot abide with any twoness. Since a not-twoness that stands opposed to twoness constitutes another duality, genuine non-duality must also encompass the duality of twoness and not-twoness, a fact that is well expressed by DeMartino's term *nondualistic-duality*. This thought is also explained in many philosophical treatises of Indian and Chinese Buddhism.

The theme of "beyond" or "going beyond"[1]—a theme that is frequently mentioned in Chan texts and is prominent in Yunmen's *Record*—addresses just this nondualistic-duality. Since one aims at leaving behind *any* duality, even nothing (which is opposed to something) is still too much:

> A monk asked Master Zhaozhou, "How is it when a man brings nothing with him?"
> Zhaozhou replied, "Throw it away!"
> The monk inquired, "Since I have nothing on me, what could I throw away?"

---

[1] Ch. *xiangshang,* Jap. kōjō. See also section 7, p. 89, note 1, and section 210, p. 190, note 5.

The Teaching of Master Yunmen

> Master Zhaozhou said, "Well, then go on carrying it!"[1]

Yunmen also criticizes holding on to "not being attached to anything," or to the one who is not holding on:

> The other religion's adherent answered: "What I regard as essential is not to be taken in by anything."
>
> Master Yunmen said in place of the Buddha: "Your turn!" (Section 194)

In true non-duality, all chains and attachments are removed, be it to "supreme wisdom" or "delusion," "Buddha" or "Mara," "sacred" or "profane," "something" or "nothing." Thus Master Linji states:

> A clear-eyed follower of the Way beats both Buddha and [the opposing force, the demon] Mara. As long as you love the sacred and hate the secular, you float in the sea of life-and-death.[2]

Questions about "going beyond the Buddha and the founders," which are frequently encountered in our text, must be seen in the same context, along with the many questions and challenges that refer to ordinary objects such as Yunmen's staff.

> I used to say that all sounds are the Buddha's voice, all shapes are the Buddha's form, and that the whole world is the Dharma body. Thus I quite pointlessly produced views that fit into the category of "Buddhist teaching." Right now, when I see a staff, I just call it "staff," and when I see a house, I just call it "house." (Section 207)

---

[1] Case 277 of Zen Master Dōgen Kigen's *Three Hundred Koans* (Sanbyakusoku).

[2] *Record of Linji*, T47: 498a28–b1.

Thusness

The passage just cited points to the "thusness" of things—the way they are when they are not seen by a self-centered and demanding "I." Exactly because the "I" is unable to see it that way, a master can say: "If you know this staff, you know everything there is to learn in life."[1] For the same reason Master Yunmen could throw a piece of wood on the floor and exclaim: "All Buddhist scriptures explain just this!" (section 274). Those who are caught in the veil of Maya—the duality of "I" and "other"—can forever know the staff or any other object only the way it is for them. Thus they are unable to respond to the following challenge by Master Yunmen:

> Yunmen held up his staff and asked, "What is this? If you
> say it is a staff, you go to hell. If it isn't a staff, what is it?"
> (Section 174)

The reason for this inability to respond is indicated once more in the following anecdote:

> Master Yunmen once seized his staff, banged it down on
> the seat and said, "All sounds are the Buddha's voice, and
> all forms are the Buddha's shape. Yet when you hold your
> bowl and eat your food, you hold a 'bowl-view'; when
> you walk, you hold a 'walk-view'; and when you sit you
> have a 'sit-view.' The whole bunch of you behaves this
> way!" (Section 171)

But one who has broken through such clinging and has become one with things without being identical with them—one who has awakened to the nondualistic-duality of the true self and thus

---

[1] *Blue Cliff Record,* case 31, T48: 171b16–17.

to the "true as-it-is-ness" or "true thusness" (Ch. *zhenru*, Jap. *shinnyo*) of all things—such a person does not live up in the clouds, immersed in past experiences and in expectations for the future and desires by the million. He lives right here and now.

> Master Yunmen said: "When a patch-robed monk sees this staff, he just calls it a staff; when he walks, he just walks; and when he sits, he just sits. In all of this he cannot be stirred." (Section 167)

As shown beautifully in the last of the "Ten Ox-herding Pictures,"[1] the awakened person does not remove himself from daily life; rather, he dives right into the middle of it and enters the bustling marketplace. Yunmen expresses this so:

> When Master Yunmen went to see Tiantong, Tiantong said, "Have you managed to settle it?"
>
> Master Yunmen asked back, "What are you saying, Reverend?"
>
> Tiantong replied, "If you *haven't* understood, then you're involved in all that is in front of you."
>
> Master Yunmen said, "If you *have* understood, then you're involved in all that is in front of you!" (Section 284)

This "involvement," however, is not the clinging embroilment of the "I":

> It may assert in unconditional affirmation, "I am" and "I am not," "I am I" and "I am not I," "I am I because I am

---

[1] This series of pictures (of which several sets with varying numbers of pictures exist) illustrates the search for one's true self through the process of finding, taming, riding, and finally forgetting a water buffalo. The series referred to here is shown and translated in D. T. Suzuki's *Manual of Zen Buddhism* (New York: Grove Press, 1978), pp. 127–34.

not I," "I am not I, therefore I am I." Unconditional Self-affirmation is, in fact, an unconditionally dynamic Self-affirmation-negation, or, Self-negation-affirmation.[1]

If this sounds abstract, it can also be formulated quite concretely: "I am I," "you are you," "I am you," "you are I." Or, with one word: love[2]—which is, again in DeMartino's words, nothing other than "the not-twoness of two" or nondualistic-duality. Though many of Yunmen's utterances (for example his calling the Buddha Shakyamuni's body "a dry piece of shit"[3]) may sound rather different, they come down to the same thing. One of the most beautiful descriptions of a selfless, awakened self is encountered in case 80 of the *Blue Cliff Record:*

> An adept of this kind can't be fooled at all—as before, mountains are mountains and rivers are rivers. He is without artifice and without clinging thoughts. He is like the sun and moon moving through the sky without ever stopping and without saying, "I have this rank and am called like that." He is like the sky everywhere covering, like the earth everywhere supporting: since they have no mind, they bring up and nurture myriad beings without saying, "I have so many accomplishments." Since sky and earth are mindless, they last forever—what has mind has limits. A person who has attained the Path is like this, too. In the midst of no activity, he carries out his activities, accepting all unfavorable and favorable circumstances with a compassionate heart.[4]

---

[1] DeMartino, "The Human Situation and Zen Buddhism," p. 170.

[2] Ibid.

[3] Section 85.

[4] *Blue Cliff Record,* case 80, T48: 206b26–c4. The translation stems, except for

Paradox

The paradoxical logic of nondualistic-duality runs through Chan texts and other Buddhist literature like a red string through Chinese coins. One of the best known examples stems from the *Diamond Sutra* and was cited by Yunmen in the following way:

> All objects (dharmas) are no-objects; just this is called "all objects." (Section 275)

The *Blue Cliff Record* features a more concrete example:

> An adherent of another faith asked [Kanadeva], "Who is in the tower ringing the bell?"
>> Kanadeva said, "A heavenly being (deva)."
>> The heretic inquired, "Who is the heavenly being?"
>> Kanadeva said, "I."
>> The adherent asked, "Who is 'I'?"
>> Kanadeva said, "I am you."
>> The adherent said, "Who is 'you'?"
>> Kanadeva said, "You are a dog."
>> The adherent said, "Who is the dog?"
>> Kanadeva said, "The dog is you."[1]

Many paradoxical statements of Master Yunmen must be seen in this light: for instance, the famous statement that what transcends Buddha and patriarchs is a flatcake (section 58), or the following passage from one of his talks (section 22):

> However, when someone gets there, speaking about fire does not burn his mouth. He can discuss the matter all day long without it ever touching his lips and teeth and with-

---

one minor modification, from Thomas and J. C. Cleary's *The Blue Cliff Record* (Boulder, Col., and London: Shambhala, 1977), p. 520.

[1] *Blue Cliff Record,* case 13, T48: 54a15–19.

out uttering a single word. Though he eats and all day long
wears his robe, he never touches a single grain of rice nor
a single thread.

From the point of view of the Chan master, such statements are
simply expressions of actualized not-twoness. For one caught in
duality, however, it may appear as complete nonsense, or alternatively as a Chan statement that poses a challenge—a challenge
that, as is often said, stands like a mile-high iron wall that gives
absolutely no hold to the dualistic mind-set.

Ways of Teaching

Many talks and dialogues that are translated in this volume are
indeed such walls, which cannot be scaled by an "I" caught up
with itself and its objects. Like so many other Chan teachers,
Yunmen was an expert at throwing the members of his audience
back on themselves, at removing all their props, and at making
them confront the fundamental contradiction inherent in being
a person. While during early Chan times we still find many intellectual discussions and set dialogues that rely on canonical scriptures, masters of the classical age (at whose end Yunmen was
living) developed a whole arsenal of new teaching devices. We
read, for example, of Master Juzhi (Jap. Gutei), who during his
whole teaching career answered any and all questions simply by
raising his finger; or of Master Deshan, who went after visitors
with his staff the moment they entered; or of Master Linji, who
frequently shouted at and slapped his students. Teaching was not
at all restricted to ritual situations created for that purpose but
could occur any time, place, or occasion.

The development of such new teaching methods is of great
importance in the history of Chan, since they not only gave the
movement a distinct identity vis-à-vis other Buddhist traditions
but also created the foundation for some of the characteristic

pedagogic directions that Chan took in the post-classical age. Indeed, unlike most other "mystical" movements, such as the medieval German mysticism of Meister Eckehart and his followers, Chan developed very effective strategies for guiding students, some of which (though modified in various ways) survive even today.

The most important of these strategies is undoubtedly the systematic use of koans. Master Yunmen can be regarded as the grandfather of this method of teaching and practicing, which was developed during the Song era, particularly through the influence of Master Yuanwu Keqin (Jap. Engo Kokugon, 1063–1135) and his disciple Dahui Zonggao (Jap. Daie Sōkō, 1089–1163). Koan use became central not only in Korean Son but also in Japanese Zen (especially but not exclusively in the Rinzai branch) and it now also flourishes in many Western Zen monasteries and centers. Yunmen used hundreds of stories and remarks from Zen history as challenges to the audience. For example, he often confronted his audience right at the outset of a talk with a statement such as "I put the whole universe on top of your eyelashes in one fell swoop" and immediately continued fanning the flame of doubt by presenting the initial statement as a challenge in koan-style:

> You all heard me say this, yet I haven't the faintest hope
> that one of you will get all worked up, step forward, and
> give me a good hard whack. Well, take your time and
> examine in detail whether you have [the entire universe
> on your eyelashes] or not! What does it mean? (Section 46)

In this example we observe another characteristic that distinguishes Yunmen from other Chan teachers: while earlier Chan dialogues for the most part consist of questions by students and answers by teachers, Yunmen constantly posed questions to his audience. He not only did so during formal talks or customary question-answer sessions but also made ample use of this teaching method during work and a variety of daily activities. Rather than just asking the type of set question—such as "Where do you come from?"—that other masters (including his teachers Muzhou and Xuefeng) were fond of, Yunmen posed questions about all kinds of topics. He was able to turn *any* situation or *any* saying into an ultimate challenge for his students. While other great Chan teachers had the same ability, Yunmen was particularly creative in applying it.

Moreover, instead of simply quoting Buddhist scriptures or other masters to support his argument, he questioned or criticized these (and of course also his own teachings) in sometimes shocking ways. His listeners were, just as his readers in the past and present, all too willing to simply accept these teachings and build their worldview cozily around them—something Yunmen tried to prevent at all cost. Thus he undercut the reliance of his students by remarks such as "I only know how to eat and drink and shit. What else would I be good for?"[1] He also generated doubt about the teachings of his predecessors; for example:

> Master Yunmen cited a saying by the Third Patriarch:
>> When mind does not arise, the myriad things have no fault.
>
> Master Yunmen said, "That's all he understood!" (Section 157)

The *Record* is full of examples where, as in this one, Yunmen uses sayings of his own or of other masters and immediately turns them into a challenging question to his audience by simply adding a concise comment. Thus Yunmen stands at the origin of a practice that most Chan masters adopt to this day, namely, that of adding short comments to stories or quotations.

---

[1] Section 144.

The Teaching of Master Yunmen

Master Yunmen mentioned the following anecdote:

>When Yunyan was sweeping the floor, Daowu said to him: "What good is so much petty effort?"
>
>Yunyan replied, "You ought to know that there is one who doesn't [make such a useless effort]!"
>
>Daowu said: "Well, that's already a second moon!"
>
>Yunyan held up the broom and said, "Which moon is this?"
>
>Daowu shook his sleeves and went out.

Master Yunmen remarked, "When a slave meets his peer, they commiserate each other." (Section 221)

Such "capping phrases," called *jakugo* or *agyo* in Japan, have since become a prominent feature of Chan/Son/Zen literature and practice. Though they also have the quality of notes or comments, their primary thrust is pedagogical. In other words, although such capping phrases are also self-expressions of the master making them, they are openly offered as a challenge to the audience or readership.

The popularity of such phrases was boosted by a descendant in Yunmen's line, Master Xuetou Chongxian (Jap. Setchō Jūken, 980–1052), who compiled an early koan collection and added his own poems to each koan,[1] and especially by Master Yuanwu Keqin (Jap. Engo Kokugon, 1063–1135) who provided introductions and commentaries to the koans and capping phrases to Xuetou's poems. The result of this labor, the *Blue Cliff Record,* became a model for a number of later koan collections and set a trend for Chan, Son, and Zen practice. It is certainly no coincidence that two noted teachers who admired Yunmen above all other masters (and practiced with koans by Yunmen

---

[1] This text, Xuetou's hundred cases with verse commentary, forms the core of the *Blue Cliff Record.*

when breaking through) also became trendsetters for koan prac-
tice in their countries and beyond: Master Dahui Zonggao (Jap.
Daie Sōkō), who was Yuanwu's disciple and the central figure in
the adoption of koan practice in China and Korea,[1] and Master
Daitō (1282–1337), who "marks the beginning of koan Zen in
Japan."[2]

However, as the following example from the *Blue Cliff
Record* clearly shows, Yunmen was fixated neither on using such
sayings nor on any particular situation:

> Xianglin [Yuan] stayed at Yunmen's side for eighteen
> years; time and again Yunmen would just call out to him,
> "Attendant Yuan!" As soon as he responded, Yunmen
> would say, "What is it?" At such times, no matter how
> much Xianglin spoke to present his understanding and
> gave play to his spirit, he never reached mutual accord
> with Yunmen. One day, though, he suddenly said, "I un-
> derstand." Yunmen said, "Why don't you say something
> above and beyond this?" Xianglin stayed on for another
> three years. A great part of the verbal displays of great abil-
> ity which Yunmen accorded in his room were designed to
> make his attendant Yuan able to gain entry and function
> anywhere.[3]

Like other Chan masters, Yunmen made vigorous use of
physical action (beating, chasing the students out of the hall, hit-

---

[1] See, for example, Cleary, *Swampland Flowers.*

[2] Seizan Yanagida, *Rinzai no kafū* (The Characteristic Style of the Rinzai Tradition) (Tokyo: Chikuma shobō, 1967), p. 173. Kenneth Kraft has described
Master Daitō and his position in the development of Japanese Zen in *Eloquent
Zen: Daitō and Early Japanese Zen* (Honolulu: University of Hawaii Press,
1992). The book includes a number of Daitō's capping phrases.

[3] *Blue Cliff Record,* case 17, T48: 157a28 ff.

ting with his staff on objects, etc.). Unlike most others, he also acted out scenes, like the one about Guanyin buying a cake in section 149 or the following:

> Addressing the assembly, Master Yunmen said, "Look, look! I got killed!"
>
> Pretending to collapse, he said, "Do you understand?" (Section 237)

A method of Yunmen which no one else has used to such effect consists of challenging his students and then, when nobody could live up to the challenge, answering his own questions in place of the person(s) questioned.[1] Such remarks frequently demonstrate both his deep insight into the hearts of men and his keenness to use all possible means in order to drive his students on in their search. In many cases, Yunmen's comments give voice to the secret thoughts, aspirations, and fears of his audience and contain a good measure of humor, often laced with irony. Such comments are prototypes of comments on koans that became popular in koan collections in the century after Yunmen's death.

Another teaching method Yunmen has been particularly celebrated for is the "one-word barrier." This is a one-word answer to a question posed by a student or, on occasion, by himself. Such answers seem wide open to various interpretations, yet as soon as one tries to approach them they appear, in Master Yuanwu's words, "like an overhanging cliff ten thousand fathoms high" or "like a million men in battle line with no place for you to get in."[2]

---

[1] See sections 222 to 263 and the survey of the content of the *Record* in the Materials section.

[2] *Blue Cliff Record,* case 14, T48: 54c27 ff.

> Someone asked Master Yunmen, "What is the eye of the genuine teaching?"
>
> The Master said, "Fu!" (Everywhere!)[1]

Such answers have also been characterized as "hammerheads with no hole."[2] Like the question "What is it?," they form the subject matter of many a koan and were later frequently used as teaching devices by other masters. These one-word answers are one of the "newly established devices of Yunmen," which he used in order to "pull out nails and wrench out pegs for people."[3] This statement, which comes from the pen of the main commentator of the greatest koan collection, indicates once more how seminal the influence of Yunmen on the Song masters who further shaped Chan methodology must have been. Indeed, many of the greatest masters after Yunmen (such as Yuanwu's disciple Dahui in China and the famous masters Daitō and Hakuin in Japan) were struggling with Yunmen's "hammerheads with no hole" before breaking through all dualistic barriers.

> Yunmen holds the world fast without the slightest leak; he cuts off the myriad flows [of delusion] without keeping a drop. Open your mouth and you're wrong. Hesitate in thought and you missed.[4]

A great intensity is apparent in many of the master's talks and dialogues; one often imagines him shouting rather than talking, and the vulgar element in his language and the con-

---

[1] See section 14 and its footnotes.

[2] *Blue Cliff Record*, case 14, T48: 154c3.

[3] This is a characterization by Master Yuanwu (*Blue Cliff Record*, case 6, T48: 146a25 ff.).

[4] *Blue Cliff Record*, case 86, T48: 211b10–11.

stant threat of physical aggression (beating, spitting, etc.) only serve to reinforce this impression. No evasion or hesitation is allowed, and all responses to the master's challenges must be spontaneous and come from the guts rather than from the brain. But hardly any of the master's disciples ever managed to get anything but abuse. Yunmen was a master of verbal devices, and his use of irony and sarcasm may be unsurpassed in Chan history. He had such a powerful arsenal of weapons that John C. H. Wu characterized his way of teaching as a "blitzkrieg" even more terrible than that of the famous Master Linji (Rinzai):

> Linji (Rinzai) only kills those whom he happens to encounter. Yunmen's massacre is universal. He does away with all people even before they are born. To him the "True Man of No Title" is already the second moon, therefore a phantom not worth the trouble of killing. Yunmen seldom if ever resorts to shouts or beatings. Like a sorcerer he kills by cursing. His tongue is inconceivably venomous, and, what makes the case worse, he is the most eloquent of the Chan masters.[1]

After Yunmen's death his teachings were often described with these three statements:
1. they permeate heaven and earth;
2. they follow the waves and adapt to the currents;
3. they cut through all streams [of delusion].[2]
The first appears to describe the encompassing and penetrating nature of his teachings; the second, the master's ability to adapt

---

[1] John C. H. Wu, *The Golden Age of Zen* (Taipei: United Publishing Center, 1975), pp. 212–13. My translations show that Yunmen resorts to beating quite frequently.

[2] *Blue Cliff Record*, case 14, T48: 154c8–10.

his teaching immediately and totally to the state and conditions of his audience; and the third, his great effort to cut off radically even the slightest trace of duality.

Whatever one could add about the content of Yunmen's teachings, one thing is abundantly clear: the so-called healthy reason of man appears to be at a loss, and this is due not to chance but to the reasons outlined above. Their aim is exactly to help in breaking through all dualistic barriers and thus to awaken to that which can never be mediated and is the most immediate.

> Yunmen asked Caoshan: "Why is it that one does not know of the existence of that which is most immediate?"
>
> Caoshan: "Just because it is the most immediate!"
>
> Yunmen: "And how can one become truly intimate with it?"
>
> Caoshan: "By not turning towards it."
>
> Yunmen: "But can one know the most immediate if one does not face it?"
>
> Caoshan: "It's then that one knows it best."
>
> Yunmen consented: "Exactly, exactly!" (Sect. 282)

Master Yuanwu, who collected the cases of the *Blue Cliff Record* and wrote comments on them, said about Yunmen's teaching: "Yunmen makes founder all those who cling to interpretations in order to make sense of him."[1] So what can one ultimately do to make sense of such teachings? Master Yuanwu says it very clearly:

---

[1] *Blue Cliff Record*, case 39, T48: 177c17.

The Teaching of Master Yunmen

You must realize that what is at stake here does not reside in words and phrases: it is like sparks from struck flint, like the brilliance of flashing lightning. However you manage to deal with this, you cannot get around losing your body and life.[1]

---

[1] Ibid., T48: 177c8–10.

Steeply Mt. Yunmen rises
Leaving the white clouds way below
Its streams rush so swiftly
That no fish dares to linger

A stream on Mt. Yunmen and a poem
(T47: 553b20)

· · ·
Talks
and
Dialogues
· · ·

Corresponding to the Occasion

■ ■ ■

1

Having come to the Dharma Hall [to instruct the assembly],[1] the Master remained silent for a long time and then said:

"The knack[2] of giving voice to the Dao is definitely difficult to figure out. Even if every word matches it, there still are a multitude of other ways; how much more so when I rattle on and on? So what's the point of talking to you right now?[3]

---

[1] In this text, formal lectures to the assembly by the master are usually introduced by this expression. Such discourses were formal in the sense that in principle all monks of a monastery (and often also visitors) were expected to be present when the master, seated on a wide chair on an elevated platform, addressed them.

[2] The term *ji* (here rendered as "knack") covers a broad spectrum of meanings such as trigger (of an event), operating mechanism, ability, knack, force, moving power, device, occasion, etc. The following passage from the *Collection from the Founder's Halls,* 3.23, 7 ff., illustrates an aspect of the knack in question here:

A monk asked, "The Ancients said that the Dao is beyond words. But if the Dao is beyond words, who is able to establish this?"

Master Yungai Zhiyuan replied, "Borrowed words give voice to the Dao; the Dao does not verbalize itself."

[3] The first speech of Master Linji (Rinzai) strikes a similar note (*Record of Linji,* T47: 496b11–14; Sasaki translation, p. 1):

"Though each of the three collections of Buddhist teaching[1] has its specific sphere—the vinaya pertains to the study of monastic discipline, the sutras to the study of meditative concentration, and the treatises to the study of wisdom—the five vehicles of the three-part Buddhist canon and the eight teachings of the five periods[2] really all boil down to just one thing, namely, the one vehicle.[3] It is perfect and immediate[4]—and extremely difficult to fathom. Even if you could understand it right now, you'd still be as different from this patch-robed monk as earth is from heaven. If in my assembly someone's ability is manifested in a phrase,[5] you'll ponder in vain. Even if, in order to make

Today, I, this mountain monk, having no choice in the matter, have perforce yielded to customary etiquette and taken this seat. If I were to demonstrate the Great Matter in strict keeping with the teaching of the Patriarchal School, I simply couldn't open my mouth and there wouldn't be any place for you to find footing.

[1] Traditionally, the written teachings of Buddhism are classified in three "baskets" (Pali: *pitaka*): monastic rules *(vinaya),* sutras, and treatises *(shastras).*

[2] The commentary in the *Collection of Items from the Garden of the Patriarchs* (Zuting shiyuan, ZZ113: 3a18–b2) points out that Master Yunmen is here probably thinking of a classification of Buddhist teachings current in Tiantai (Tendai) Buddhism. Such classifications were attempts to bring consistency and continuity to Buddhist teachings by attributing them to specific phases and occasions of the Buddha's life.

[3] The singular or unique vehicle (ekayāna). In the Chan movement, one's own realization of the non-dual or mindless mind (Ch. *wushin,* Jap. *mushin*) is regarded as the one vehicle.

[4] Various interpretations of the Chinese word *dun* (here rendered by "immediate") have been advanced in specialist literature. I translate it by "immediate" because this suggests both a temporal dimension ("sudden") and the lack of any mediation.

[5] The great number of Chan stories and exchanges where some expression of one's understanding is requested attest to the importance of such verbal manifestations of ability in the form of words. See also the end of section 22.

progress, you sorted out all Chan teachings with their thousand differences and myriad distinctions, your mistake would still consist in searching for proclamations from other people's tongues.

"So how should one approach what has been transmitted? By talking in here about 'perfect' and 'immediate'? By [this] here or [that] there?[1] Don't get me wrong: you must not hear me say this and then speculate that 'not perfect' and 'not sudden' are it!

"There *must* be a real *man* in here! Don't rely on some master's pretentious statements or hand-me-down phrases that you pass off everywhere as your own understanding! Don't get me wrong. Whatever your problem right now is: try settling it just here in front of the assembly!"

At the time Prefectural Governor Ho was present. He performed the customary bow and said, "Your disciple requests your instruction."

The Master replied, "This weed I see is no different!"[2]

2

545b2–5

An official asked, "Is it true that the Buddha Dharma is like the moon in the water?"[3]

---

[1] "Here" and "there" as a pair subsume poles of duality such as delusion and enlightenment, ordinary and holy, imperfect and perfect, mediated and unmediated (immediate), etc.

[2] Since in Chan texts "weed" is used as a metaphor for illusions which the teacher steps into in order to save his disciples (see, for example, section 147), Yunmen possibly is saying: "You're quite an ordinary weed, just like the others here; so what I said about settling your problem in front of everyone applies to you, too!" The answer may also mean: No special treatment here!

[3] The teachings of the Buddha and of the Chan masters are regarded as aids that can, depending on the circumstances (which change like waves in the water), take on various forms. All teachings point towards one's own awakening (the moon); one is thus warned not to mistake the teaching device (the pointing

The Master replied, "[Even] a pure wave has no way of penetrating through [to the moon]."

The official pressed on, "By what way did you reach it, Reverend?"

The Master answered, "Where did you get this second question from?"[1]

The official went on, "How about my situation right now?"[2]

The Master said, "The road across this mountain pass is totally blocked!"

545b8–10

3

Someone asked Master Yunmen, "Since antiquity, the old worthies have transmitted mind by mind.[3] Today I ask you, Master: What device do *you* use?"

The Master said, "When there's a question, there's an answer."[4]

---

finger, or in this case the reflection of the moon in the water) for the ultimate goal.

[1] See Yunmen's statement "A coin lost in the river is found in the river" (section 15). Yunmen appears to point out that the questioner's treasure lies just where his question is coming from, as in the Chan saying "One's own house-treasure is not found on the outside."

[2] The questioner wants the master to tell him where he stands on the path to the moon of awakening.

[3] "Transmitting mind by mind" is a pivotal Chan concept whose history has been traced in Isshu Miura and Ruth Fuller Sasaki, *Zen Dust* (Kyoto: The First Zen Institute of America in Japan, 1966), p. 230 ff., and in Seizan Yanagida, *Shoki zenshūshisho no kenkyū* (Kyoto: Hōzōkan, 1967), p. 471 ff. It is said to express the teaching method of the Buddha and Bodhidharma.

[4] In section 81, Yunmen replies practically in the same words to a question about teaching methods.

The questioner went on, "In this case it isn't a useless device!"[1]

The Master replied, "No question, no answer."

4

Someone asked, "What about the occasion when the hen pecks and the chick flies?"[2]

The Master said, "Crack!"

The questioner went on: "Does this apply [to me]?"

The Master said, "Slowly, slowly!"[3]

5

Someone asked, "What's my central concern?"

The Master replied, "Hey, this question really got me!"[4]

---

[1] This is probably an expression of appreciation: Your teaching won't be lost on me, I accept and appreciate it.

[2] What I translate as "filing" and "pecking" is a Chinese expression consisting of two characters; the first is an onomatopoetic rendering of the sound of filing and the second of knocking. They represent the effort of a chick to break out of its shell and of the mother hen to help it in this endeavor. This stands for the simultaneous and timely effort of teacher and student, resulting in the student's breaking out of his shell. See case 16 of the *Blue Cliff Record*.

[3] This expression was used several times by Yunmen for admonishing his disciples to take one step at a time and not to imagine having reached the end of the road before having even taken the first steps. See sections 8, 29, and 46.

[4] Literally: "I have sincerely accepted your question!" Professor Yoshitaka Iriya points out that this is likely to be a sarcastic response: "Wow! What a question!," with the undertone "This one is really much too big for you!" Additionally, there might be an element of "You're asking *me* about *your own* central concern?"

545b14–15

6

Someone asked Master Yunmen, "How about a phrase that is separately transmitted outside the written teachings?"

The Master said, "Come on, present this question to the whole assembly!"

545b15–27

7

The Master said,

"Don't say that I'm deceiving you today! I simply cannot help performing a messy scene in front of you; what a laughing-stock I'd be if some clear-sighted man were to see me! But right now I cannot avoid this.[1]

"So let me ask you all: What has so far been the matter with you?[2] What do you lack? If I tell you that nothing whatso-ever is the matter then I've already buried you; you yourself must arrive at that realization! Don't give free rein to your mouths for haphazard questioning. It's pitch-black in your hearts, and one of these days something will be very much the matter![3]

"If you're of hesitant disposition, then you might turn your sight towards the teachings of the old masters and look hither and thither to find out what they mean. You do want to

---

[1] This is an aspect of the theme treated in section 3; what is essential is self-awakening, and this cannot be mediated, just as smelling and tasting cannot be conveyed.

[2] The *Record of Linji* is on the same line:

Followers of the Way, right now the resolute man knows full well that from the beginning nothing is the matter. Only because your faith [in this] is insufficient do you ceaselessly chase about; having thrown away your head you go on and on looking for it, unable to stop yourself (T47: 498b13–15; cf. Sasaki translation, p. 13).

[3] This is likely to be an allusion to death.

attain understanding, don't you?! The reason [you're unable to do so] is precisely that your own illusion accumulated since innumerable eons is so thick that when in some lifetime you hear someone talk [about the Dharma], you get doubts. Seeking understanding by asking about the Buddha and his teaching, about *going beyond* and *coming back* [into the conditioned],"[1] you move further and further away from it.[2] When you direct your mind towards it, you've gone astray; how much more so if you use words to describe it?[3] What if 'not directing one's mind' were it? Why, is anything the matter? Take care!"[4]

---

[1] The two concepts *xiangshang* and *xiangxia* literally mean "up," "upward," "beyond," "ascending," and "down," "downward," "descending" and were quite popular in Chan circles around Yunmen's time. They have the connotation of rising above *(xiangshang)* everything that is conditioned (including the Buddha and his teaching)—the central task of the practitioner intent on achieving liberation from the shackle of duality, and thus naturally also a core theme of Yunmen's teaching and Chan teaching in general—and coming back down *(xiangxia)* into the realm of the conditioned (the world of illusion, discrimination, and attachment). The downward movement is characteristic of the activity of the teacher who uses all kinds of devices as skillful means (see section 183). See also section 147, p. 157, note 1, and section 210, p. 190, note 5.

[2] All such seeking is still directed towards objects rather than the questioner himself; in this sense such a seeker is "looking south to see the Great Bear [in the northern sky]" (see also section 113).

[3] Compare Master Linji's words (*Record of Linji,* T47: 496b25–c1; cf. Sasaki translation, p. 2):

> But the instant you open your mouth you are already way off. Why is this so? Don't you know? The venerable Sakyamuni said: "The essence of my teaching is separate from words, because it is neither subject to causation nor dependent on conditions." Your faith [in this] is insufficient, that's why I have bandied words today.

[4] This expression was often used by Chan masters at the end of formal talks to their community. Just like the English equivalent, it can be both used as an ordinary farewell formula and invested with more meaning.

545b28–29

8

Someone asked, "What tune do you sing, Master?"[1]

The Master replied, "The twenty-fifth of the twelfth month!"[2]

"What if I sing it?"

"Slowly, slowly!"

545b29–c1

9

Someone asked, "What did the Patriarch intend in coming from the West?"

Master Yunmen replied, "That's as clear as day!"

545c4

10

Someone asked, "What is the way beyond?"[3]

The Master said, "Nine times nine is eighty-one."[4]

545c4–6

11

Someone asked, "What is my 'I'?"

The Master said, "It's strolling in the mountains and enjoying the rivers."

---

[1] What is it that you have to say; what is your message?

[2] This is the time just before a year's end; the expression may correspond to our "it's the eleventh hour."

[3] What is the way beyond suffering, beyond the shackles of duality? For "beyond" see section 7, p.88, note 2.

[4] Yunmen was quite fond of this expression; it occurs no less than five times in this text. Professor Iriya found that multiplication tables used in the Tang dynasty start out with this. Thus it could correspond to some very basic knowledge, something that everybody with minimal education knows. Here it may mean "first things first" or, more aggressively, "You have not even begun learning to calculate and are already talking of such big numbers?"

"And what is your 'I,' Reverend?"

The Master replied, "You're lucky that the precentor isn't here!"[1]

12

545c6–7

Someone asked, "How about [the Buddha,] the instructor?"
The Master answered, "That's too rude!"

13

545c7–8

"What is the teaching of the [Buddha's] whole lifetime?"
"Speaking in tune with any particular [occasion]."[2]

14

545c8

Someone asked Master Yunmen, "What is the eye of the genuine teaching?"[3]

The Master said, "It's everywhere!"[4]

---

[1] The precentor is the monk in charge of general affairs who also assigns the duties within the monastery and dispenses punishment (including physical beating; see Holmes Welch, *The Practice of Chinese Buddhism,* 1900–1950 (Cambridge, Mass.: Harvard University Press, 1967), p. 67 *et passim*).

[2] This short exchange forms case 14 of the *Blue Cliff Record,* where Master Yuanwu stresses in his comments that in transmitting this teaching one must take the time and conditions into account.

[3] "Eye" signifies the core or essence of something. Both the Chinese master Dahui Zonggao and the Japanese master Dōgen Kigen chose this expression (literally, "treasury of the eye of the genuine teaching") as titles of their central works.

[4] This is one of Master Yunmen's famous one-word answers. In the original, the character in question has meanings such as: 1. vast, great; and 2. general, universal; all, everything, everywhere. Translators including myself must capitulate, in part because of Yunmen's intentional use of multiple meanings. Dai-

545c9–10

15

Someone asked: "What does 'Sitting correctly and contemplating true reality'[1] mean?"

The Master said, "A coin lost in the river is found in the river."[2]

545c10–11

16

Someone asked Master Yunmen, "What is the monk's practice?"

The Master replied, "It cannot be understood."

The questioner carried on, "Why can't it be understood?"

"It just cannot be understood!"

545c12–16

17

A monk inquired, "What is the meaning of the [Buddhist] teachings?"

The Master asked back, "What sutra are you reading?"

---

setz T. Suzuki renders this word as "Everywhere!" (*Essays in Zen Buddhism, First Series,* p. 352), Charles Luk as "Universality" (K'uan-yü Lu, *Ch'an and Zen Teachings, Second Series* [London: Rider, 1961], p. 203), John Wu as "All-comprehensive!" (*Golden Age of Zen,* p. 220), Thomas and J. C. Cleary as "Universal" (*Blue Cliff Record,* p. 39), and Wilhelm Gundert as "Common! [i.e., everybody has it though it is the most unfathomable mystery]" (*Bi-yän-lu: Meister Yuan-wu's Niederschrift von der Smaragdenen Felswand* [Frankfurt/M.: Ullstein Verlag, 1983], p. 150). See also section 18, where Yunmen answers the same question in a more definite manner.

[1] "Sitting correctly" signifies genuine meditation in which everything is seen as it really is (Jap. *sono mama*)—i.e., in its true reality.

[2] See Master Linji (*Record of Linji,* T47: 497b16–18):
   If you wish to differ in no way from the Patriarch-Buddha, just don't seek outside. The pure light in your every thought is nothing other than the Dharmakāya-Buddha within your own house.

The monk replied, "The *Wisdom Sutra.*"

The Master cited: " 'All knowledge is pure.' Have you seen this even in a dream?"

The monk said, "Let's leave 'All knowledge is pure' aside: what is the meaning of the teachings?"[1]

The Master replied, "If in your heart you had not failed someone, you would not be blushing! But I spare you the thirty blows of the staff [you deserve]."[2]

545c17

18

Someone asked, "What is the eye of the genuine [teaching]?"[3]

Master Yunmen said, "The steam of rice gruel."[4]

545c17–18

19

Someone asked, "What is perfect concentration (samadhi)?"

The Master replied, "Shut up unless I ask you!"

---

[1] The reaction of Master Yunmen suggests that the monk blushed while he asked this.

[2] This phrase was frequently employed not only by Yunmen but also by his teacher Muzhou to scold monks. Thirty blows of the staff constitute a very harsh punishment. The master's reaction can certainly be regarded as lenient ("I see that you are blushing and have recognized your fault, so I won't strike you"), but there might also be a razor-sharp edge to it: "This kind of behavior is usually subject to harsh punishment—but for what I see here I wouldn't even lift my hand!"

[3] In section 14, Yunmen answers the same question differently.

[4] Gruel is a broth made from two to three parts of rice to seven or eight parts of water. This conjee was served for breakfast. Monastic regulations allowed only one more meal before noon (*zhai,* usually rice and vegetables).

545c18–19

20

Someone asked, "What is the place from whence all the buddhas come?"

Master Yunmen said, "[Where] the East Mountains walk on the river."[1]

545c19–20

21

Someone said, "Please, Master, show me a way in!"

The Master said, "Slurping gruel, eating rice."

545c20–
546a5

22

The Master said,

"I have no choice;[2] if I tell you that right now nothing is the matter, I have already buried you. However much you want to make progress and seek intellectual understanding by looking for words and chasing after phrases and setting up questions and inquiries by means of a thousand differences and myriad distinctions: it just brings you a glib tongue and leads you further and further from the Way. Where is there an end to this?

---

[1] A key to this exchange may lie in a poem by the Buddhist layman Fu Dashi (see note to section 170). It is found in the *Record of the Mirror of the Teachings* (Ch. Zongjinglu, Jap. Sugyōroku; T48: 448a21–23):

> [Where] the East Mountains float on the river and the West Mountains wander on and on, in the realm [of this world?] beneath the Great Dipper: just there is the place of genuine emancipation.

[2] Other Chan masters see themselves in a similar bind; Master Linji, for example, began his very first sermon with these words (T47: 496b12; Sasaki translation, p. 1):

> Today, I, this mountain monk, having no choice in this matter, have perforce yielded to customary etiquette and taken this seat.

"If this very matter could simply be found in words—the three vehicles' twelve divisions of teachings certainly do not lack words, do they?—then why would one speak of a 'transmission outside the scriptural teachings'?[1] If wisdom were a function of studying interpretations, it would merely be like that of the saints of the ten stages who, though disseminating the Dharma as [plentifully as] clouds and rain, were still severely reprimanded [by the Buddha] because they perceived their self-nature as if through a veil of gauze. Hence we know that any kind of 'having mind'[2] is as far away [from what is at stake here] as the sky from the earth.

"However, when someone gets there, speaking about fire does not burn his mouth. He can discuss the matter all day long without it ever touching his lips and teeth and without uttering a single word. Though he eats and all day long wears his robe, he never touches a single grain of rice nor a single thread.[3]

"Anyway, this is still only *talk* about our teachings; but you must really *make them yours!* If within these walls a phrase packs a punch, then you will ponder in vain. Even if you can accept some statement as you hear it, you're still daydreamers."

At the time a monk asked, "How about such a phrase?"

The Master replied, "Brought up."

23

546a5–7

Someone asked, "What is 'being silent while speaking'?"

The Master said, "A clear opportunity just slipped through your fingers!"

---

[1] See Introduction, p. 12.

[2] The Chinese character for "heart" or "mind" *(xin)* stands here for the deluded subject that experiences physical and spiritual objects, the "I" that faces any "other." See Introduction, p. 41 ff.

[3] See p. 67 ff.

The questioner went on, "And what is 'speaking while being silent'?"

The Master said, "Oh!"[1]

The questioner continued, "What is it like when one is neither silent nor talking?"

With his staff the Master drove the questioner out of the hall.

546a7–8

24

Someone asked, "What is Yunmen's sword?"

The Master said, "Founder."[2]

546a8–9

25

Someone asked, "What is the place from which all buddhas come?"[3]

Master Yunmen said, "Next question, please!"

---

[1] An expression of doubt or surprise. This character can also be read "sha," in which case it would stand for an exclamation without specific meaning: "Shaaaa!" or "Shhhh!"

[2] This could also mean "founders"; the Chinese text here allows no differentiation between singular or plural modes. However, it is likely that instead of the dead founders of Chan, the text points at "the living patriarch" of whom Master Linji said (*Record of Linji*, T47: 499c12; Sasaki translation, p. 20): "Your minds and Mind do not differ—this is called [your] Living Patriarch." The sword that takes and gives life stands for the Chan teaching whose objective is the death of the self-attached "I" and the awakening of the "living patriarch" (True Self) of each person. Thus Yunmen's co-disciple Xuansha says (*Extensive Record of Xuansha*, ZZ126: 179b7): "[The sword] is just *you*, the very *you* that does not understand!" See also Yoshitaka Iriya's translation, *Gensha kōroku*, vol. 1 (Kyoto: Zenbunka kenkyūjo, 1987), p. 77.

[3] See the virtually identical question and Yunmen's different answer in section 20.

26

Someone asked Master Yunmen, "What is the absolute concentration which comprehends every single particle of dust?"

The Master replied, "Water in the bucket, food in the bowl."

27

"How about the place of non-thinking?"

The Master replied, "Cognition can hardly fathom it."[1]

28

"How about when one makes a hole in the wall in order to steal the neighbor's light?"[2]

"There it is!"[3]

---

[1] Both question and answer stem from the *Inscription on Trusting in Mind* (Xinxinming, T51: 457b17–18):

> *The realm of non-thinking*
> *can hardly be fathomed by cognition;*
> *in the sphere of genuine suchness*
> *there is neither "I" nor "other."*

[2] Kuang Heng, prime minister under emperor Yuan Di of the former Han period and famous commentator on Confucian canonical literature, is said to have been so keen on learning as a poor student that he "stole" the neighbor's light. This stands for an extraordinary effort. Here, both question and answer appear focused on the light of which Master Linji says (T47: 497c4–7; cf. Sasaki translation, p. 9):

> Followers of the Way, mind is without form and pervades the ten directions. In the eye it is called seeing, in the ear hearing, in the nose it smells odors, in the mouth it holds converse, in the hands it grasps and seizes, and in the feet it moves and runs. Fundamentally it is a single subtle radiance, divided into six sensory perceptions. Yet since this mind is nothing, one is free, wherever one is!

[3] Both in the sense of "Exactly!" and "Here it is, shining brightly!" See again the *Record of Linji* (T47: 497b16–20; cf. Sasaki translation, p. 8):

29

The Master said,

"All twelve divisions of the three vehicles' teachings explain it back and forth, and the old monks of the whole empire grandly proclaim, 'Come on, try presenting to me even a tiny little bit of what it all means!': all of this is already medicine for a dead horse.

"Nevertheless, how many are there who have come even that far? I don't even dare to hope for an echo of it in your words or a hidden sharp point in one of your phrases.

> *A blink of an eye—a thousand differences.*
> *When the wind is still, the waves are calm.*[1]

May you rest in peace!"[2]

30

Someone asked, "What is the fundamental teaching?"
Master Yunmen said, "No question, no answer."[3]

If you wish to differ in no way from the Patriarch-Buddha, just don't seek outside. The pure light in your every thought is nothing other than the Dharmakâya-Buddha within your own house. . . . This threefold body is nothing other than you who are listening to my discourse right now before my very eyes.

[1] The *Record of the Mirror of the Teachings* (Zongjinglu; T48: 430c4–5) says: Mind and its objects condition each other . . . like the water which forms waves depending on the winds.

[2] A pious enunciation used at Chinese funerals, here probably used in an ironic sense.

[3] See section 3 for another example of this answer.

31

Someone asked Master Yunmen, "How about: 'The Triple World[1] is but mind, and the myriad things are but consciousness'?"[2]

The Master said, "Today I don't answer any questions."

The questioner insisted, "Why don't you answer any questions?"

The Master said, "Will you understand it in the year of the donkey?"[3]

32

Someone asked Yunmen, "What is the sword [so sharp that it cuts even] a hair blown [over its blade]?"[4]

The Master said, "Chop!"

He added, "Slash!"[5]

---

[1] The three aspects of desire, form, and formlessness are said to characterize the whole object-world of the human being.

[2] This was in Chan literature a much quoted saying of Vijñaptimātra flavor. This Buddhist religio-philosophical movement asserted that without a subject ("mind" or "consciousness") there is no object ("Triple World") and vice versa. See also section 77.

[3] Since no such year exists in the Chinese year-cycle, this means in effect "You'll never ever understand it!"

[4] The sword is in Chan literature commonly associated with the Chan or Buddhist teaching and teaching method in general (as in "the sabre that kills and the sword that gives life"; see also note to section 24). The sword mentioned here was famous for being so sharp that it cut even a hair blown across its blade.

[5] Two onomatopoetic renderings were proposed by Professor Iriya, the first standing for the sound of cutting bone and the second for that of slicing flesh. See the answer that Yunmen's co-disciple Xuansha gave to the same question (*Extensive Record of Xuansha*, ZZ126: 179b7):

[The sword] is just *you*, the very *you* that does not understand!

33

Someone asked, "What is the inward-and-outward radiance?"[1]

Master Yunmen asked back, "In what direction is your question pointed?"

The questioner said, "What is reaching the light?"

The Master asked, "If someone suddenly asked you this, what would you say?"[2]

The questioner continued, "How about after reaching the light?"

The Master replied, "Forget the light; give me first the reaching!"

34

Someone asked Master Yunmen, "What is the most urgent phrase?"

The Master said, "Eat!"

---

[1] This question probably refers to a verse ascribed to Master Tanxia Tianren (739–824). Tanxia spoke about the wondrous pearl in each person which is hard to find but can be intimately perceived in the Sea of the Buddhist Teaching and then went on to say (*Jingde chuandenglu,* T51: 463b16–18; see also section 245):

> This pearl constantly moves around within the five components (skandhas) of each living being, showing and hiding itself, and its inward and outward radiance is of great supernatural power. Neither large nor small, it shines day and night and illuminates everything—yet when one looks for it, it is no thing and leaves no trace.

[2] This appears to be one more attempt by Yunmen to tell the questioner that, since his own radiance is in question, no one else should be qualified to answer this question.

35

Someone asked, "What is the original mind?"
The Master said, "You've raised it; it's quite apparent!"[1]

36

Someone asked Yunmen, "What is the essence of a patch-robed monk?"
The Master said, "It's your turn!"[2]
The questioner insisted, "Please, Master, tell me!"
The Master said, "I'm playing the harp for an ox!"[3]

37

Having entered the Dharma Hall Master Yunmen said:
"Brothers! You certainly have visited many regions searching for knowledge in order to settle [the problem of] life-and-death;[4] and everywhere you went there must have been masters who gave you expedient words of compassion. Now is there any statement of theirs that you could not penetrate? Come forward

---

[1] Cf. the verse cited in *Collection from the Founder's Halls,* 1.38:
Just your mind is the original mind, and this original mind is not something.

[2] This expression is used as in a board game: This is your move, it's up to you!

[3] Yunmen could as well talk to a wall. Did he not already say that the answer to this question can come only from the questioner himself?

[4] Life-and-death circumscribes the basic framework of human life: having to live and having to die. This is what every person starts out with and has to deal with in one way or another; in the first of his Four Noble Truths, the Buddha called this "suffering." See p. 37.

and try relating it, so that I can discuss it with all of you! Anything? Anything?"

Just when a monk who had stepped forward was about to ask a question, the Master said: "Go! Go! You're further than a hundred thousand [miles] from the road to India."[1]

With that the Master left his seat.

546b19–20

38

Someone asked Master Yunmen, "What is most urgent for me?"

The Master said, "The very *you* who is afraid that he doesn't know!"[2]

546b20–22

39

Someone asked, "What is the mooing of the clay ox of the snow peak?"[3]

The Master said, "Mountains and rivers are running away!"

"And how about the neighing of Yunmen's wooden horse?"

Master Yunmen replied, "Heaven and earth black out."

---

[1] This could also signify "the road to the Western Paradise," i.e., the paradise of Amitabha Buddha. However, in this case it may simply mean: "Way off the mark!"

[2] This answer occurs one more time in the *Record of Yunmen* (T47: 553b3), that time in response to the question: "What is my self?"

[3] Mooing clay oxen, neighing wooden horses, laughing stone men, blinking corpses, and other paradoxical creatures are common in Chan texts as symbols of the paradoxical teaching of the Buddha (who is said to have taught on the snow peaks of the Himalayas) and of the masters.

40

Someone asked Master Yunmen, "How about doing as one pleases?"[1]

The Master said, "It's your turn!"

41

Having entered the Dharma Hall, Master Yunmen said:

"If, in bringing up a case I cause you to accept it instantly, I am already spreading shit on top of your heads.[2] Even if you could understand the whole world when I hold up a single hair, I'd still be operating on healthy flesh.

"At any rate, you must first truly attain this level of realization. If you're not yet there, you must not pretend that you are. Rather, you ought to take a step back, seek under your very feet, and see what there is to what I am saying!

"In reality, there is not the slightest thing that could be the source of understanding or doubt for you. Rather, you have the one thing that matters, each and every one of you! Its great function manifests without the slightest effort on your part; you are no different from the patriarch-buddhas![3] [But since] the root of

---

[1] Literally, "seven lengthwise, eight across." This expression is also found in secular literature describing mighty warriors who have mastered the technique of handling a sword and are capable of using it without contraint.

[2] See also section 175.

[3] This could also be translated as "patriarchs and buddhas." The *Record of Linji* has several almost identical formulations (T47: 497b8; 497c1; 502a13). The one that is most strikingly similar to the present passage reads:

> This very you standing distinctly before me without any form, shining alone—this can expound the Dharma and listen to it! Understand it this way, and you are not different from the Patriarch-Buddha. (T47: 497b28–c1; Sasaki translation, p. 9)

your faith has always been shallow and the influence of your evil actions massive, you find yourselves all of a sudden wearing many horns.[1] You're carrying your bowl bags[2] far and wide through thousands of villages and myriads of hamlets: what's the point of victimizing yourselves? Is there something you all are lacking? Which one of you full-fledged fellows hasn't got his share?[3]

"Though you may accept what I am saying for yourself, you're still in bad shape.[4] You must neither fall for the tricks of others nor simply accept their directives. The instant you see an old monk open his mouth, you tend to stuff those big rocks right into yours, and when you cluster in little groups to discuss [his words], you're exactly like those green flies on shit that struggle back to back to gobble it up! What a shame, brothers!

"The old masters could not help using up their whole life-time for the sake of you all. So they dropped a word here and half a phrase there to give you a hint. You may have understood these things; put them aside and make some effort for yourselves, and you will certainly become a bit familiar with it. Hurry up! Hurry up! Time does not wait for any man, and breathing out is

---

[1] Horns are in Chan literature often associated with dualistic attachment or delusion in general, as are weeds. Cf. *Blue Cliff Record,* case 95 (T48: 218a19–21): "Where there is a buddha, you must not stay; if you do, horns sprout. Where there is no buddha, quickly run past; if you don't, the weeds will be ten feet high."

[2] These bags were used by monks to carry their begging bowl and a few other possessions around on pilgrimage.

[3] See *Record of Linji,* T47: 499c10 (Sasaki translation, p. 20):
> The non-dependent man of the Way who right now before my eyes is listening to my discourse, clearly distinguishable, [it is you who've] never yet lacked anything."

[4] Or: out of luck.

no guarantee for breathing in again! Or do you have a spare body and mind to fritter away? You absolutely must pay close attention! Take care!"

42

546c19–21

Someone asked: "What is the primary phrase?"

The Master said, "Nine times nine is eighty-one."[1]

The monk bowed.[2]

The Master said, "Come here!"

The monk stepped in front of the Master. The Master struck him.

43

546c23–27

Someone asked, "I heard a teaching that speaks of the purity of all-encompassing wisdom. What is that purity like?"

Master Yunmen spat at him.

The questioner continued, "How about some teaching method of the old masters?"

The Master said, "Come here! Cut off your feet, replace your skull, and take away the spoon and chopsticks from your bowl: now pick up your nose!"

The monk asked, "Where would one find such [teaching methods]?"

The Master said, "You windbag!" And he struck him.

---

[1] See section 10, note 4.

[2] The monk expresses his gratitude and acceptance of the master's teaching—which is not at all what Yunmen wants.

44

Someone asked Master Yunmen, "What is Chan?"
    The Master replied, "That's it!"
    The questioner went on, "What is the Dao?"
    The Master said, "Okay!"[1]

45

Someone asked: "How about 'all things are the Buddha Dharma'?"
    The Master replied, "The grannies of a three-house hick town crowd the city crossing. Do you understand?"
    "No."
    The Master said, "You're not the only one who does not understand; there's definitely someone else who doesn't!"[2]

46

Having entered the Dharma Hall, Master Yunmen said:
    "I put the whole universe on top of your eyelashes in one fell swoop."[3]
    "You all heard me say this, yet I haven't the faintest hope that one of you will get all worked up, step forward, and give me a good hard whack. Well, take your time and examine in detail whether you have [the entire universe on your eyelashes] or not! What does it mean?

---

[1] Yunmen's answers often simply confirm the quality of a question and push the student to pursue it thoroughly by himself.

[2] In his retirement lecture, Professor Iriya took this conversation as an example of how Yunmen often attacks the Buddha or other Chan teachers in a sarcastic and seemingly irreverent manner.

[3] See section 99.

Corresponding to the Occasion

"Even though you may manage to understand this in here: as soon as you join my assembly, you get beaten up so much that your legs break. The moment you hear me say that there's a sage at work somewhere, you should spit me full in the face and offend my eyes and ears. But since you're not up to that, you immediately accept whatever people say. This already falls into the category of secondary action.[1]

"Haven't you heard that the instant Deshan[2] saw a monk enter the gate, he took up his stick and drove him away? And Muzhou,[3] seeing a monk come in through the gate, said: 'It's a clear case,[4] but I spare you the thirty blows [you deserve]!'[5]

"And how should one deal with the rest? With this bunch of windbags who gulp down other people's pus and slobber, can recall heaps and loads of rubbish, and display their donkey lips and horse mouths everywhere, boasting: 'I can ask questions in five or ten alternative ways'? Even if you ask questions from morning till evening with the answers taking you into the night: Will you ever see anything, even in a dream? How will you apply your strength for the benefit of others?

"You resemble those people who, when someone invites the monks to a donated feast, say: 'The food is fine, but what's

---

[1] These are not one's own realizations but rather reactions to what others have realized. Such secondhand realizations are not "one's own house-treasure," a fact that a master immediately sees, as the examples that follow show.

[2] Deshan Xuanjian (780–865), the teacher of Yunmen's master Xuefeng Yicun (822–908).

[3] Muzhou, Yunmen's first Chan teacher. See p. 19.

[4] Ch. *xianzheng gongan*, Jap. *genjō kōan*. This is the original meaning of this expression, which acquired much fame, especially after Dōgen used it in the title and as the theme of the first chapter of his major work *Shōbōgenzō*. It means "a clear case," as when someone is caught in the act while committing a crime.

[5] See section 17, note 2.

there to talk about [with the donor]?' Some day you'll be facing the King of Hell, Yama[1]—and he won't accept your glib talk!

"My brothers, if there is one who has attained it, he passes his days in conformity with the ordinary. If you have not yet attained it, you must at any price avoid pretending that you have. You must not waste your time, and you need very much to pay close attention!

"The old men definitely had some word-creepers[2] which could be of help. For instance [my teacher] Xuefeng said: 'The whole world is nothing but you.' Master Jiashan said: 'Get hold of me on the tips of the hundred grasses, and recognize the emperor in the bustling marketplace.' Master Luopu said, 'The moment a single grain of dust arises, the whole world is contained in it. On [the tip of] a single lion's hair the whole body of the lion appears.'

"Anyway, try to get a firm hold [on the meaning of these sayings], pondering them from all angles—and after days or years an entrance will open up by itself! This matter does not allow anyone to step in for you; it is nothing but each person's very own mission. If some old monks come out into the world, it is just to act as witness for you. If you have found some entrance or some clue, you shouldn't lose sight of yourself. If as a matter of fact you haven't attained it yet, no methods applied [by a teacher] will be of any use.

"My brothers, you who all in the same way wear out your straw sandals on pilgrimages and turn your back on teachers and

---

[1] Yamarāja. This figure has different roles in the Vedic, Brahmanic, and Buddhist traditions; in the last, he is the terrible King of Hell, the underworld administrator presiding over the judgment of the dead.

[2] Words are in the Chan tradition often called "creepers" because people trip over them and get caught up in them.

parents—you absolutely must fix your eyeballs directly on this! If you have not yet found any clue but have met an undisguised skillful [master who goes after you] like a dog that bites a boar, and who doesn't care about his own life and won't shy away from going through mud and water for you, and if he has something good for chewing: then blink your eyes and raise your eyebrows, hang your bowl bag high [on the wall], and for ten or twenty years exert yourself to the utmost! Don't worry about not bringing your effort to completion: should it happen that you do not yet achieve it in this lifetime, you will not fail to get a human body in the next one, and then it will turn out that you have saved labor with regard to this teaching. Thus you will not idly squander your whole life, and you will also not let down the patrons of Buddhism, your teachers, and your parents.

"You must be cautious! Don't idle away your time bumming around in the provinces and loitering in the districts, wandering thousands of miles with your staff across your shoulders, spending a winter here and a summer there, enjoying the beautiful mountains and rivers and doing whatever you feel like, being provided with plenty of donated food and easily obtaining worldly possessions. What a shame that is, what a shame! [You know the proverb:] 'Wanting to get himself one peck of rice he ends up losing six months' provisions.' What is the use of such pilgrimages? How dare you consume the faithful almsgiver's bunch of vegetables or even a single grain of his rice?

"You must see for yourself! There is nobody to stand in for you, and time does not wait for anyone; one day [you'll be about to pass away and] your gaze will fall on the earth. How will you manage from then on? You must not resemble a crab that, dropped into hot water, flails its legs in a frenzy! Big words won't help you much there, you windbags!

"Don't carelessly fritter away your time. Once you lose your human body you won't regain one for countless eons. This is no trifling matter! Don't rely on anything present. If even a secular man said, 'Should I hear about the Way in the morning, I will die content in the evening':[1] how much more so we monks? What is the problem we ought to deal with? You must make a great effort! Take care of yourself!"

547b24–27

47

Someone asked, "How about 'giving life'?"

"If you had not failed someone in your heart, [you would not blush]."[2]

"And how about 'taking life'?"

"One must not auction off a monk's possessions for three days after his death."[3]

"What if one neither gives nor takes life?"

Master Yunmen chased the questioner out of the hall with his staff.

547b28–c1

48

Someone asked, "If one kills one's father and mother, one can repent in front of the Buddha. Where does one repent if one kills the Buddha and the patriarchs?"

The Master said, "Exposed!"[4]

---

[1] This quotation is from the fourth section of Confucius' *Analects*.

[2] At other occasions (T47: 545c15 and 546b24), Yunmen uses the full form of this saying (here added in brackets).

[3] The possessions of a monk were auctioned off after his death in order to cover medical and burial expenses. As in his first reply, Yunmen appears to criticize the monk for not being in the position to truly ask this question.

[4] The same one-word answer appears also later in the *Record of Yunmen* (T47: 566c14): "The Master once said, 'What is a phrase that is in accord with understanding?' On behalf [of the silent audience] he replied, "Exposed!' "

49

547c1–2

Someone asked, "Is anything amiss when one does not even give rise to a single thought?"

The Master replied, "[As much as] Mt. Sumeru."[1]

50

547c2–3

Someone asked, "What is the characteristic style of your teaching, Master?"

"May a scholar come and tell you!"

51

547c4–5

Someone asked, "Life-and-death is here; how am I to cope with it?"

The Master said, "Where is it?"

52

547c11–15

Having entered the Dharma Hall for a formal instruction, Master Yunmen said:

"You monks must not think falsely; heaven is heaven, earth is earth, mountain is mountain, river is river, monk is monk, and layperson is layperson."[2]

---

[1] This is the mythical mountain of gigantic proportions that is thought to form the center of the earth.

[2] See the words of Master Qingyuan in the *Compendium of the Five Lamps* (Wudeng huiyuan, ZZ138: 335a9 ff):

> Thirty years ago, before I practiced Chan, I saw that mountains are mountains and rivers are rivers. However, after having achieved intimate knowledge and having gotten a way in, I saw that mountains are not mountains and rivers are not rivers. But

After a long pause he said, "Come on, try picking up that hill for me!"

Then a monk asked, "What is it like when I see that mountain is mountain and river is river?"

The Master said, "Why does the triple monastery gate pass through [this hall] here?"

The monk continued, "If that is so I'm no more deluded now."

The Master said, "Give me back your words!"[1]

547c16–18

53

Having entered the Dharma Hall for a formal instruction, Master Yunmen said after a long silence:

"Is there anybody at all who can say it?[2] Let the one who can step forward!"

The assembly remained silent.

The Master picked up his staff and said, "[My challenge] before was a small trench full of shit, and [the lifting of my staff] right now is a big one."

The Master stepped down from his seat.

---

now that I have found rest, as before I see mountains as mountains and rivers as rivers.

[1] The monk can keep his words "mountain is mountain and river is river" only when he sees the monastery gate pass through the hall.

[2] With Dōgen—who devoted chapter 39 of his Shōbōgenzō to this theme—this ability of expression acquired overtones that were not present in China. There this expression had, like many others in Chan literature, both a common and a religiously loaded meaning. Questions like "Where are you from?" or "How are you?" and phrases such as "Take care of yourself!" belong to this category. Here, Yunmen does not just ask "Can you tell me?" but challenges his disciples: "Are you able to express your [awakened] self?"

54

547ι18–19

Someone asked, "The myriad things come to one. Now I do not ask about the one but rather: what are the myriad things?"

Master Yunmen said, "You came in here to bandy words and to cheat me!"

55

548a2–4

Someone asked Yunmen, "I did all I could and came here. Will you accept?"

The Master said, "Nothing wrong with this question!"

The questioner went on, "Leaving aside this question: will you accept?"

The Master said, "Examine carefully what you first said!"

56

548a8–11

Having entered the Dharma Hall for a formal instruction, Master Yunmen said:

"Today I shall bring up a case [from the Chan tradition] for you."

The whole assembly listened attentively. After a while a monk stepped forward and bowed. When he was about to ask a question, Master Yunmen went after him with his staff, crying: "You resemble those exterminators of Buddhism, those monks who receive donated food on the long bench[1] [and say] 'What's there to talk about [with the donor]?' You bunch of rowdies!"

Using his staff, Master Yunmen chased them out of the hall at once.

---

[1] This was a platform inside the Monks' Hall on which five to ten people could meditate.

113

57

Someone asked Yunmen, "Now that the whole assembly has gathered like clouds, what will you talk about?"

The Master said, "The text that follows is too long. Let's postpone it to some other day!"

The questioner continued, "How about leaving it at that?"

The Master said, "Trapped."

"Where am I trapped?"

Master Yunmen said, "As soon as you've gorged food on the long bench you tell fibs."

58

Having entered the Dharma Hall, the Master said:

"Even if a word, the very instant it is brought up, puts the thousand differences into a single groove and includes the minutest particles, it is still but an expression of salvational teaching. What then is a patch-robed monk supposed to say? If he discusses in here what the patriarchs and the Buddha meant, the Sixth Patriarch's unique way will be leveled. But is there anyone who can put it right? If there is, come forward!"

At the time a monk asked,[1] "How about saying something that transcends the buddhas and goes beyond the patriarchs?"

The Master said, "Sesame flatcake."[2]

The monk went on: "What's the connection?"

The Master said, "Exactly! What's the connection?!"

---

[1] The present exchange forms case 77 of the *Blue Cliff Record* (T48: 204b11).

[2] As I learned from Victor Mair, this is a baked flatcake four to six inches in diameter, made from wheat flour dough, baked plastered against the inner side of an earthen oven, and sprinkled with sesame seeds. This is one of the most celebrated instances in Chan literature of presenting everyday reality as the highest doctrine.

Corresponding to the Occasion

The Master thereupon said, "Without having understood a thing, you ask about statements that transcend the buddhas and patriarchs the moment you hear people talk about the intent of the patriarchal teachers. What are you calling 'buddha,' and what are you calling 'patriarch' when you speak about statements that transcend the buddhas and go beyond the patriarchs? And when you ask about the escape from the three realms (of sensuous desire, form, and formlessness): bring me these three realms! Is there [a perceptive faculty such as] seeing, hearing, feeling, or knowing to stop you? And what object of perception is agreeable to you? Do you come to terms with some [teaching] vessel? And what do you regard as differentiating views?[1]

"What can the sages do when you puff yourselves up [and say]: 'My whole body is nothing but truth,' and 'All things exhibit the essence'? This is out of your reach. And when I say to you 'Right now, is anything the matter?,' I have already buried you. If you really don't have any clue, then for a time go into yourself and investigate thoroughly on your own: What, besides wearing a robe, eating, moving bowels and urinating, is the matter?[2] What's the use of giving rise to so many kinds of delusive thoughts without any reason?

"Again, there's a bunch of people who casually gather in groups, manage to quote some sayings of the ancients, try to

---

[1] Professor Iriya thinks that the Chinese text of these last few sentences might be corrupt; the translation of this passage is tentative. However, the tenor of Yunmen's words seems clear enough: he attacks his students for mentioning things that they are unable to handle and challenges them to show him what they are talking about.

[2] Cf. *Record of Linji*, T47: 498a16–17:
> Followers of the Way, the Buddhist teaching does not necessitate any effort. Just be ordinary and without concern—defecating, urinating, putting on clothes, eating food, and lying down when tired.

See also the slightly different version in Sasaki's translation, pp. 11–12.

memorize them, evaluate them with their delusive thoughts, and say: 'I have understood the Buddhist teaching!' They busy themselves with nothing but discussions and while away their days following their whims. Then they come to feel that this does not suit their fancy; they travel through thousands of villages and myriads of hamlets and turn their backs on their parents as well as their teachers. You're acting in just this way, you bunch of rowdies. What is this frantic pilgrimage you're engaged in?"

And the Master chased them out with his staff.

548b22–24

59

Someone asked Yunmen, "[It is said that] one should not leave home [to become a monk] without one's parents' consent. How would one then be able to leave home?"

The Master said, "Shallow!"

The questioner said, "I do not understand."

The Master remarked, "Deep!"

548c1–3

60

Someone asked Master Yunmen, "What is it like when all powers are exhausted?"

The Master said, "Bring me the Buddha Hall; then I'll discuss this with you."

The questioner asked, "Isn't that some different matter?"

The Master shouted, "Bah! Windbag!"

548c8–16

61

Having entered the Dharma Hall for a formal instruction, Master Yunmen said:

"It is well known that shallowness [of virtue] is the trend of these times, and that this generation is living at the end of the imitation period of Buddhism;[1] so nowadays, when monks go north, they call this 'worshiping Mañjushrī,'[2] and when they go south they say they 'journey to Nanyue.'[3] [People who] go on such pilgrimages, though styled 'mendicant monks,' just squander the alms of the faithful.[4] What a shame! What a shame! When asked they turn out to be [as ignorant as] lacquer is black; they just pass their days following their whim. If there are some of them who, by learning like crazy and informing themselves widely, manage to absorb some sayings and are looking everywhere for similar words, they get approved as venerables and

---

[1] The second of three periods of Buddhist teaching that were distinguished in China: 1. The period of the correct or real teaching (500 years after the Buddha's death); 2. The period of the semblance or imitative teaching (the following 1000 years); 3. The period of the end of teaching (the following 3000 years). Though Buddhist doctrine and practice do exist in the second period, they only bear resemblance to the true kind; thus the result of true practice and basis of true teaching, awakening, is said to be lacking.

[2] The bodhisattva of Wisdom, one of the most important figures of the Buddhist pantheon. The most famous site of Mañjushrī (Ch. Wenshu, Jap. Monju) worship in China was Mt. Wutai (Wutaishan), situated near the northeastern border of Shansi province. Sasaki (*Record of Linji,* pp. 74–75, note 89) explains:

Mañjushrī Bodhisattva was believed to appear frequently on the mountain to teach the Dharma, and thousands of monks as well as common people would make pilgrimages there to pay homage to him.

[3] The Nanyue (or Hengyue) mountain range, situated in the Hengzhou prefecture of Hunan province, was famous as the place of residence of such celebrated Chan masters as Nanyue Huairang (677–744) and Shitou Xiqian (700–790).

[4] Master Linji chimes in (T47: 498c26–29; Sasaki translation, p. 16):

There's a bunch of students who seek Mañjushrī on Wu-t'aishan. Wrong from the start! There's no Mañjushrī on Wu-t'aishan. Do you want to know Mañjushrī? Your activity right now, never changing, nowhere faltering—this is the living Mañjushrī.

lightly dismiss superior men, thus creating karma of misfortune.[1]

"Don't say, when some day the King of Hell, Yama, pins you down, that nobody warned you! Whether you are an innocent beginner or seasoned adept, you must show some spirit! Don't vainly memorize [other people's] sayings: a little bit of reality is better than a lot of illusion. [Otherwise,] you'll just go on deceiving yourself.

"What is the matter with you?[2] Come forward [and tell me]!"

548c16–17

62

Someone asked Master Yunmen, "I am definitely on the wrong track. Please, Master, give me some instruction!"

The Master said, "What are you talking about?"

548c17–18

63

Someone asked, "What is the meaning of [Buddhist] teaching?"

The Master said, "The answer is not finished yet."

The questioner asked, "What did your answer consist in, Master?"

The Master said, "Oh, I thought you were smart . . . !"

---

[1] Yunmen is not alone in warning against these dangers; Master Linji issues the same warning (T47: 498b20–22; Sasaki translation, p. 14):

> Followers of the Way, don't have your face stamped at random with the seal of sanction by an old master anywhere, then go around saying, 'I understand Ch'an, I understand the Way.' Though your eloquence is like a rushing torrent, it is nothing but hell-creating karma.

[2] As in several other passages (e.g., sections 7 and 58), Yunmen asks his students to stop running after the sayings and insights of others and to face their own situation, their "reality": Is anything the matter with you? If yes, what is it?

64

548c18–20

Someone asked, "What is the true essence of monkhood?"

Master Yunmen said, "You monk over there, step forward!"

The monk in question stepped forward.

The Master said, "Bah! Get out!"

65

548c20–21

"How can I understand your one phrase, Master?"

"It's the twenty-fifth day of the twelfth month!"[1]

66

548c21–22

"I am not questioning you about the core of Buddhist doctrine but would like to know what stands at the center of our own tradition."

The Master replied, "Well, you've posed your question; now quickly bow three times!"[2]

67

548c24–26

Someone asked, "How is the buddha-and-patriarch-illness[3] to be healed?"

"Find out what's wrong, and it will all come together."

"How is it to be healed?"

"Fortunately you're strong!"

---

[1] Hurry up, there is hardly any time left.

[2] Bowing three times is a sign of gratitude for a received teaching. By asking the monk to bow, Yunmen breaks off this conversation.

[3] See the remarks about the bodhisattva illness in section 98, note 3.

68

The Master entered the Dharma Hall for a formal instruction. When the assembly had gathered and settled, he took his staff, pointed in front of him and said:

"All the buddhas of the whole universe, numberless as specks of dust, are all in here, disputing the Buddhist teaching and trying to win the argument. Now is there anyone who can dissuade them? If nobody is up to it, let me try doing it for you."

Thereupon a monk said, "Please, Reverend, dissuade them!"

The Master said, "You're a bunch of wild fox ghosts!"[1]

69

Someone asked, "What is it like when everything is swallowed up in one gulp?"

The Master said, "Then I am in your belly."

"Why would you be in my belly, Master?"

The Master replied, "Give me back your words!"[2]

70

Having entered the Dharma Hall for a formal instruction, Master Yunmen said after a long silence:

"This compromises me very much!"[3] And he stepped down from his seat.

---

[1] In East Asia, foxes are said to have various magical powers; they can, for example, transform themselves into beautiful femmes fatales. In Chan, this expression is used for criticizing impostors. See also sections 91 and 146.

[2] This answer implies that the questioner was not yet in the position to ask his first question.

[3] Professor Iriya compares this to the story where Baizhang sat one night inside the Dharma Hall and suddenly spat on the floor. To his disciples' question

71

549b4–8

Having entered the Dharma Hall for a formal instruction, Master Yunmen said:

"I've said what there was to say. . . ."

A monk stepped forward, bowed, and wanted to pose a question. Master Yunmen took his staff and hit him, saying: "What good can you tell from bad? You bunch of rowdies! You're all like this monk; how dare you receive the faithful offerings of the almsgivers! The sentient beings with bad karma are all in here—and what dry piece of shit are they seeking to chew?"

And Master Yunmen chased all the monks at once out of the hall with his staff.

72

549b10

Someone asked Master Yunmen, "What is Chan?"

The Master said, "Is it all right to get rid of this word?"

73

549b14–15

Someone asked Master Yunmen, "What is the original source?"[1]

The Master said, "Whose donations do you receive?"

---

why he had done this he replied: "I was just thinking about wisdom and nirvana."

[1] In Chan literature, this expression is often used for that which underlies and grounds all phenomena, i.e., the perceiving subject. See, for instance, the *Record of Linji* (T47: 497b25; Sasaki translation, p. 8):

Virtuous monks, you must recognize the one who manipulates these reflections. He is the primal source of all the buddhas.

74

Having entered the Dharma Hall for a formal instruction, Master Yunmen said:

"You lot who get lost on pilgrimages: each and every one of you, whether you come from south of the Yellow River or north of the sea, has his native place. Now, do you know it? Give it a try, come forward and tell me—I'll check it out for you! Anybody? Anybody?

"If you don't know [your native place], then I have deceived you. Would you like to know? If your native place is in the north, there are Master Zhaozhou[1] and Mañjushrī of the Wutai mountains;[2] both are in here. If your birthplace is in the South, there are Xuefeng,[3] Wolong,[4] Xiyuan,[5] and Gushan[6] who are all in here. Would you like to get to know them? Meet them right here! If you don't see them, don't pretend that you do! Do you see? Do you? If you don't: watch me ride out astride the Buddha Hall! Take care!"

---

[1] Zhaozhou Congshen (778–897).

[2] See section 61, p. 117, note 2.

[3] Master Xuefeng, one of Yunmen's principal teachers.

[4] Several masters were called Wolong, but as Yunmen means to mention well-known figures it seems most likely that he here thinks of Master Anguo Huiqiu (d. 913), a successor of Yunmen's older co-disciple Xuansha Shibei (835–908).

[5] Again, there are a number of masters who were referred to by this temple name. The master in question may be Xiyuan Daan (793–883), Dharma heir of Baizhang.

[6] Probably Gushan Shenyen (862–938), a Dharma heir of Yunmen's teacher Xuefeng Yicun.

75

549c10–11

Someone asked Yunmen, "What is 'Form is nothing other than emptiness'?"[1]

The Master said, "The staff is hitting your nose."

76

549c15–16

A monk asked, "What is mind?"[2]

The Master said, "Mind."

The monk went on, "[I] don't understand."

The Master said, "[You] don't understand."

The monk asked, "So what is it after all?"

The Master replied, "Bah! Take a walk in a quiet spot wherever you like!"

77

549c16–18

Someone asked: "What is it like when [one realizes that] the three realms[3] are nothing but mind, and the myriad things are merely [produced by one's] cognition?"[4]

The Master replied, "Hiding in one's tongue."[5]

---

[1] This is part of the central statement of the famous *Heart Sutra:* "Form is nothing other than emptiness, and emptiness nothing other than form."

[2] Ch. *xin,* Jap. *kokoro;* see section 22, p. 95, note 2.

[3] The realms of sensuous desire, form, and formlessness.

[4] This expresses the central tenet of the "idealist" school of Buddhist thought (Vijñaptimātra, i.e. "Consciousness Only" or better "Representation Only.").

[5] It is possible that the tongue stands for "words"; indeed, there is an instance in the *Record of Yunmen* (562b4–5) where Yunmen speaks of "hiding in words":
> Once [Master Yunmen] said, "Is there one who is hiding himself in words?" In place [of his audience] he remarked, "Got it!"

"And what is that like?"
The Master said, "Su-lu, su-lu."[1]

549c26–27

78

Having entered the Dharma Hall for a formal instruction, Master Yunmen said:

"I let you talk as much as you like. From morning till evening nobody is blocking your mouth to prevent you from speaking. Well?"

549c28–
550a3

79

Master Yunmen entered the Dharma Hall for a formal instruction, and the assembly gathered. After a long while he lifted his staff and said:

"Look, look! The people of northern Uttara-kuru[2] saw the trouble you took gathering firewood,[3] and as a present to you they're holding a wrestling bout in the monastery yard. On top of that, they are reciting for you from the *Wisdom Sutra:* "[Oh] purity of all-encompassing wisdom, non-dual, undivided, without difference, not separate. . . ."[4]

---

[1] This spell was among other things used for fending off evil spirits.

[2] The northern of the four continents around the central Mt. Sumeru. Square in shape, its people are said to be square faced. It is judged to be superior because people live one thousand years and produce food without effort.

[3] Gathering firewood was, together with other chores such as picking tea leaves, bringing in rice, and growing vegetables, one of the activities where the monks could try keeping up their meditative concentration while engaged in physical labor.

[4] This is a phrase found in many Wisdom scriptures. By reciting such profound doctrines while performing a boisterous wrestling bout, these people serve as

A monk then asked: "How about this 'purity of all-encompassing wisdom'?"

Master Yunmen said: "In India they'd cut off your head and arms;[1] here you may indict yourself and get out!"

80

Someone asked Yunmen, "What is shallowness within profundity?"

The Master said, "Mountain, river, earth."[2]

"What is profundity within shallowness?"

The Master replied, "Earth, mountain, river."

The questioner continued, "What is profundity?"

The Master said, "Going to India in the morning and returning to China in the evening."[3]

81

Someone asked Master Yunmen, "The thousand expedient means all lead back to the source. I wonder what that source is really about."

The Master said, "Where there is a question, there is an answer. Come on, say it quickly!"

The monk said, "Yes, . . ."

The Master said, "Far from it!"

---

an example to the monks who find it hard to keep their meditative concentration even while gathering wood.

[1] The commentary included in *Zuting shiyuan* (ZZ113: 5a7) says that this was the harsh punishment given to the loser of a public debate.

[2] See also section 122.

[3] For an additional example of this phrase, see section 112.

550a12–14

82

"What is the sword of Yunmen?"[1]
    "It's drawn!"
    "How about the one who is using it?"
    The Master said: "Su-lu, su-lu!"[2]

550a14–15

83

"What is the purpose of the Patriarch [Bodhidharma]'s coming from the West?"
    The Master replied, "Go ahead, tell me if there is none!"
    The questioner continued, "I don't understand!"
    The Master remarked, "That was one hell of a question!"

550a22–b5

84

Having entered the Dharma Hall for a formal instruction, Master Yunmen said:

    "I see that, in spite of my teaching on the second or third level, the lot of you are unable to get it. So what's the purpose of vainly wearing monks' robes? Do you understand? Let me explain this to you in plain terms: When at some later point you go to various places and see some Venerable lift his finger or hold up a fly-whisk[3] and say 'this is Chan' and 'this is the Dao,' you

---

[1] See also section 32.

[2] See section 77, p. 124, note 1.

[3] "A horse-tail mounted on a handle, originally used by Indian Buddhist monks to drive away insects. In the Ch'an sect, one of the insignia of office of a high ranking priest." Yoshitaka Iriya, Ruth Fuller Sasaki, and Burton Watson, "On Some Texts of Ancient Spoken Chinese" (unpublished typescript), p. 30.

ought to take your staff, smash his head, and go away! Otherwise you'll end up among the followers of Deva Mara[1] and ruin our tradition.

"If you really do not understand, look for the time being into some word-creepers.[2] I keep telling you that all the buddhas of past, present, and future from lands innumerable as specks of dust, including the twenty-eight Indian and the six Chinese patriarchs, are all on top of this staff; they expound the Buddhist teaching, manifest by virtue of their spiritual powers in different forms, and let their voices be heard at will in all ten directions, without the slightest hindrance. Do you understand? If you don't understand, do not pretend that you do. Well then: Have you closely examined what I just said and do you really see it? But even if you'd reach that plane, you still could not even dream of a true monk. You wouldn't even meet one in a three-house hamlet!"

The Master abruptly seized his staff, drew a line on the ground, and said: "All [the buddhas and patriarchs] are in here." He drew another line and said, "All have gone out of here. Take care of yourselves!"

85

Someone asked, "What is Shakyamuni's body?"
The Master said, "A dry piece of shit."[3]

---

[1] This king is one of the powerful demons of Buddhist lore; he is said to obstruct the Buddhist truth and to interfere when someone tries to do good.

[2] See section 46, p. 108, note 2.

[3] See also section 71.

550b15–16

86

Someone asked Yunmen, "Would you please, Master, tell me what the cardinal meaning of our [Chan] tradition is?"

The Master said, "In the South there's Master Xuefeng, and in the North Master Zhaozhou."[1]

550b17–19

87

Someone asked Yunmen, "Though this is constantly my most pressing concern, I cannot find any way in. Please, Master, show me a way in!"

The Master said, "Just in your present concern there is a way."[2]

550b21–22

88

"How do I actually experience the unique way of subtle power?"[3]

The Master said, "After thirty years!"[4]

---

[1] See section 74 for notes about these teachers. There is one more instance of this answer, in section 134; that question addresses the central concern of a monk. The implication seems to be: "I will not tell you; you had better ask one of the most famous teachers!" (However, there is an example of a teacher who responded to such a question with "I have a headache, I'll tell you another time!") See also sections 71 and 94.

[2] See the story of the encounter of Shin'ichi Hisamatsu with Bernard Phillips on p. 51.

[3] Here and in the following exchange, this expression *(xuanji)* appears to refer to a power or activity available to an accomplished teacher, a power that he also applies in dispensing appropriate instruction. The student thus asks: "How can I get awakened?"

[4] Thirty years is, according to Professor Iriya, a common unit of practice; it corresponds roughly to the number of years one can devote to religious practice in one lifetime. Yunmen may thus say that this power can be realized only after a lifetime of arduous practice.

89

550b24–25

"What is it like when neither the subtle power [of awakening] nor [any objects that] strike the eye will do?"

The Master replied, "Overturn this statement!"[1]

90

550b27–29

Having entered the Dharma Hall for a formal instruction, Master Yunmen said:

"The Bodhisattva Vasubandhu has transformed himself quite pointlessly into this wooden staff."

Then he drew a line on the ground with his staff and said: "All ye buddhas, countless like grains of sand: go ahead, entangle yourselves in words in here!"

With this the Master left his seat.

91

550c1–4

In the Dharma Hall, Master Yunmen said:

"I will be candid with you; I know someone when I meet him.[2] But in spite of such old women's talk[3] you fail to under-

---

[1] This famous answer is a riddle; indeed, in his commentary to case 15 of the *Blue Cliff Record,* Yuanwu remarks that the point of the question was abstruse and misleading and therefore the answer had to be that way, too; Yuanwu goes on to say that Yunmen is riding the thief's horse in pursuit of the thief (T48: 155b11–12; Cleary and Cleary translation, p. 99). "Turn that statement around!" or the Clearys' "an upside-down statement" are just two possible alternative translations.

[2] Master Linji said in similar fashion: "Whoever comes to me, I do not fail him: I know exactly where he comes from" (T47: 497a5) and "Whoever comes here, whether he be monk or layman, I discern him through and through" (499a10; both translations by Sasaki, pp. 5 and 17).

[3] In Chan texts, "old women's talk" is most often used in an approving sense: extremely compassionate talk.

129

stand. You gorge yourselves every day, and after your meals you prowl up and down [from Monks' Hall to Dharma Hall]. What kind of [teaching] vessel are you looking for?[1] You pack of wild foxes! What the hell are you doing in here?"

The Master chased all the monks at once out with his staff.

550c4–6

92

Someone asked, "Fall is beginning and the [three-month] summer [training period] is at its end. If in the future someone were to suddenly question me, how exactly should I respond?"

"Get out of here, the whole assembly!"

"What did I do wrong?"

"Come on, give me back the money for ninety days' worth of food!"

550c6–7

93

"I have only recently arrived at your Dharma seat and am not yet clear about the style of your teaching."

The Master replied, "Well, what could I say without your questions!"[2]

---

[1] The implication here seems to be that after having eaten physical food the monks crave spiritual food. They ignore the grandmotherly efforts of their teacher and keep looking for something else.

[2] This question was often posed; Yunmen's answer here is made of pure acid. In another Chan text a monk asked some master about Bodhidharma's intention in coming from the West, whereupon that master said, "Oh, I would never have thought of this if you hadn't asked me!"

94

550c7–9

"[It is said:] In the countries of the ten points of the compass there is only one kind of teaching. What is this teaching?"

"Why don't you ask something else?"

The questioner said, "Thank you, Master, for your guidance."

The Master immediately shouted: "Khaaa!"[1]

95

550c19–20

Someone asked Master Yunmen, "What is it like when the tree has withered and the leaves fallen?"[2]

The Master said, "That's wholly manifest: golden autumn wind."

96

550c20–21

Someone asked Yunmen, "How about the pearl in the cloth bag?"[3]

---

[1] The shout (often rendered "katsu") was a frequently used device, especially by Master Linji and his followers. Professor S. Ueda called it a "proto-word" ("Ur-Wort")—i.e., a word before and underneath all words. See also section 145.

[2] This expression stems from chapter 25 of the *Nirvana Sutra* and appears to be a metaphor for nirvana or enlightenment. Similarly, a poem by Han Shan evokes a tree that is older than the forest it stands in; its bark is all dried up and its leaves have fallen—and only naked reality is left. At any rate, the question asks what it is like to be enlightened and sets the stage for the answer by providing the imagery of autumn.

[3] The metaphor of the pearl in a cloth bag stems from the *Lotus Sutra,* where the following story is told: Before a friend's departure for a long journey, a man hid a pearl in the seam of his friend's clothes in order to help him in times of trouble. The traveler indeed got into trouble and found the hidden pearl,

The Master said, "Can you tell?"[1]

550c21–22

97

Someone asked Master Yunmen, "What is a successor of the patriarchal tradition?"
The Master said, "Sounds good!"

550c23–26

98

Master Yunmen entered the Dharma Hall and said, "A bodhi-sattva striving for wisdom[2] must be able to know the illness of sentient beings;[3] then he will also be capable of knowing [his own illness], the illness of the bodhisattva striving for wisdom. Well, if there is someone here who can understand this, he ought to step forward and try demonstrating it to all of us!"

---

which saved him. The pearl thus stands for something very precious that we carry with us but are not aware of—i.e., buddha-nature.

[1] It's your pearl, so you ought to tell me!

[2] One who practices to attain awakening.

[3] This refers to the suffering mentioned in the first of the Four Noble Truths, which afflicts all human beings and is at root attachment (see p. 37). One who practices to attain wisdom thus attempts to get rid of this illness, but that task is easier said than done since there is not only attachment to oneself and objects, which expresses itself as greed and aversion (the illness of sentient beings), but also attachment to not having such attachments (the illness of the bodhisattvas). The beginning of the *Record of Baizhang* gives extensive explanations about these two forms of illness and about the realm of ultimate freedom beyond any attachment and non-attachment (*Baizhang guanglu*, ZZ118: 83a–b). The various forms of attachment and their elimination are also a central theme of the *Vimalakīrti Sutra*. See also Paul Demiéville's classic article on illness *(byō)* found in *Hōbōgirin: Dictionnaire encyclopédique du bouddhisme d'après les sources chinoises et japonaises* (Paris: A. Maisonneuve and Tokyo: Maison Franco-Japonaise, 1937), vol. 3, pp. 224–70.

No one in the assembly said a word.

Then the Master said, "If you cannot do that, then don't prevent me from taking a walk wherever I please!"

99

Having entered the Dharma Hall for a formal instruction, Master Yunmen said:

"Today I'm getting caught up in words with you: Shit, ash, piss, fire! These dirty pigs and scabby dogs[1] can't even distinguish good from bad and are making their living in a shit pit!

"Let me tell you: you must grasp the whole universe, the earth, the three vehicles' twelve divisions of teachings, and the verbal teachings of all buddhas of the three realms and all the masters in the whole empire at once right on your eyelashes! Even if you were able to understand this here and now, you'd still be a fellow out of luck who is jumping into a shit pit for no reason at all. If [anyone like that] should ever come by my assembly of patch-robed monks, I'd beat him up till his legs break!"

Three monks then stepped forth simultaneously and bowed. The Master said: "A single indictment takes care [of all three of you]."[2]

---

[1] Maybe this whole phrase should be taken literally as a strong curse: "Shit-ash-piss-fire-dirty pig-scabby dog!"

[2] Yunmen says here that all three monks committed the same crime. In the earlier stone inscription (Daijō Tokiwa, *Shina bukkyō shiseki kinenshū* [Tokyo: Bukkyō shiseki kenkyūkai, 1931], p. 113, lines 6 to 7), this last section is added in a slightly different form to a short sermon that reads:

> Once [Master Yunmen] saw the assembly gather, and after a while he said, "If you don't understand for thirty years, don't say that you didn't meet a teacher."
>
> Thereupon three monks stepped forward simultaneously and bowed.
>
> The Master said, "Three people, one warrant!"

551a4–6

100

Someone asked: "How can one quickly go beyond the three realms [of sensual desire, form, and formlessness]?"

The Master said, "How can one quickly go beyond the three realms?"

The questioner said, "That's it!"

The Master remarked, "If that is it then it's all over with you!"[1]

551a7–9

101

Someone asked Yunmen, "How about when I clear away everything in one fell swoop?"

The Master said, "What do you do about me?"

The questioner replied, "That's your problem!"

The Master exclaimed, "You windbag!"

551a9–10

102

"What is the Dao?"

The Master replied, "To break through this word."

"What is it like when one has broken through?"

"A thousand miles, the same mood."[2]

---

[1] Cf. Yuanwu's saying (*Blue Cliff Record*, T48: 177c10):
However you manage to deal with this, you cannot get around losing your body and life.

[2] This expresses the closeness good friends feel even when they are a thousand miles apart.

103

Someone asked: "An old monk said, 'I have realized the ultimate principle.'[1] What is this ultimate principle?"

The Master said: "How about what's in my hand?"

The monk insisted: "I'm asking about the ultimate principle!"

The Master hit him with his staff, crying: "Boo! Boo! Just when it's shattered, you say: 'Please teach me about it!' Wherever they go, people [like you] know just how to squeeze things into their scheme at random. Step forward and let me ask you: You're usually on the long [meditation] bench and hold discussions about 'transcending' [particulars] and 'descending' [into them],[2] and about 'going beyond the buddhas' and 'transcending the patriarchs.' Now tell me: Does a water buffalo know what 'going beyond the buddhas and transcending the patriarchs' is all about?"

The monk replied, "Just before, somebody already asked this!"[3]

The Master replied: "This [kind of phrase] is something you can learn on the long [meditation] bench. No need for someone to state the obvious and say 'it has' when it has and 'it doesn't have' when it doesn't."

The monk said: "If [the water buffalo] has [the meaning of 'transcending the buddhas and going beyond the patriarchs']: for what purpose does it then have a hide and wear horns?"

The Master said: "I *knew* you're just one who memorizes words."

---

[1] "Ultimate norm" and "the ultimate" are other possible translations.

[2] Literally, "upward" and "downward"; see section 7, p. 89, note 1.

[3] This appears to have been a set way of evading a question: "That's an old hat!"

Master Yunmen added: "Come, come! Let me ask you again: You all carry your staff across your shoulders and claim that you 'practice Chan' and 'study the Dao' and that you're searching for the meaning of 'going beyond the buddhas and transcending the patriarchs.' Well, here's my question to you: is the meaning of 'going beyond buddhas and transcending patriarchs' present [in all your actions] during the twelve periods of the day—walking, standing, sitting, lying, shitting, pissing—[and anywhere including] the vermin in the privy and the lined-up mutton traded at market stalls? If there's anyone able to tell me, he should step forward! If nobody is capable of that, don't prevent me from taking a walk [wherever I please,] east or west!"

With this, Master Yunmen left his teacher's seat.

551a26–27

104

"What was [Bodhidharma's] purpose in coming from the West?"

The Master replied, "[You must be hungry after such a long trip;] there's gruel and rice on the long bench!"

551a28–b2

105

A monk asked, "What was Bodhidharma's aim when he came from the West?"

The Master replied, "A question from you, Venerable, and I take that three-thousand-mile leap."

The monk rejoined: "Thank you, Master, for your instruction."

Master Yunmen said, "Wait, wait, tell me: what I just said to you, what does it mean?"

The monk had no answer.

The Master remarked: "Come again in thirty years; then I'll strike you thirty times with my staff!"[1]

106

551b7–9

Having entered the Dharma Hall for a formal instruction, Master Yunmen said: "The Buddha attained the Way when the morning star appeared."

A monk asked: "What is it like when one attains the Way at the appearance of the morning star?"

Master Yunmen said: "Come here, come here [I'll show it to you]!"

The monk went closer. Master Yunmen hit him with his staff and chased him out of the Dharma Hall.

107

551b10–11

Master Yunmen entered the Dharma Hall for a formal instruction.

A monk stepped forward, bowed, and said: "Please, Master, respond to our questions!"

Master Yunmen cried: "Hey, you all!"

As the members of the assembly looked up the Master at once left his seat.

---

[1] The master attempts to prevent the student from simply accepting his teaching, first by questioning him and then by calling him so immature that even after thirty years of training he would be ready only for harsh physical punishment.

551b12–13

108

Master Yunmen entered the Dharma Hall for a formal instruction. There was a long silence. Then a monk stepped forward and bowed.

The Master said: "Too late!"

The monk consented: "Yes."

The Master said: "You lacquer bucket!"[1]

551b14–17

109

Having entered the Dharma Hall for a formal instruction, Master Yunmen said: "Is there anybody who is able to pose a question? Come on, ask one!"

A monk stepped forward, bowed, and said: "Please, Master, examine [me]!"

The Master replied: "I threw in a hook to catch a giant fish—but what did I manage to catch? A frog!"

The monk said: "Make no mistake, Reverend!"

Master Yunmen said: "There you bit off more than you can chew![2] Don't you think?"

The monk was speechless.

Master Yunmen hit him.

551b20–22

110

Someone asked Yunmen, "Why does Samantabhadra ride an elephant and Mañjushrî a lion?"[3]

---

[1] Lacquer stands for pitch-black ignorance.

[2] Literally, "In the morning you [intend to] go three thousand, but in the evening you ran eight hundred." Probably a proverb. The implication seems to be that one thinks or says one can accomplish more than is actually possible.

[3] The bodhisattva Samantabhadra (Ch. Puxian, Jap. Fugen) is most often

The Master said, "I have neither an elephant nor a lion; I'm riding on the Buddha Hall and leave through the triple monastery gate!"

111

551b24–25

"What is it like when all-embracing wisdom pervades and there is no hindrance?"

The Master replied, "Clean up the ground and sprinkle it with water: His Excellency the Prime Minister is coming!"

112

551b26–29

Someone asked: "What is that which is transmitted separately from the teachings of the three vehicles?"

The Master said, "If you don't ask me I won't answer. But if you do, I go to India in the morning and return to China in the evening!"

The questioner said, "Please, Master, point it out to me!"

The Master replied, "Hopeless case!"

113

551b29–c1

"What was the intention of the Patriarch [Bodhidharma] when he came from the West?"

The Master replied, "What good is it to mumble in one's sleep in broad daylight?"

---

shown riding on an elephant, and Mañjushrī (Ch. Wenshu, Jap. Monju) on a lion.

551c4–5

114

"What is the fundamental meaning of Buddhist teaching?"

The Master said, "You're facing south to see the Great Bear!"[1]

551c6–7

115

A monk asked, "What is the characteristic style of your house, Master?"

The Master replied, "Monk, you took the vows much too soon!"

551c10–11

116

Someone asked Yunmen, "Ever since I came to your Dharma seat, Master, I just don't understand. Please impart me your instruction!"

The Master said, "May I lop off your head?"[2]

551c11–12

117

Someone inquired, "Please, Master, instruct me; make me get rid of confusion once and for all!"

---

[1] Since one must face north in order to see the Great Bear constellation, this means "to take a completely wrong approach," "to be totally on the wrong track."

[2] In commenting upon this exchange, Professor Iriya refers to a story about a previous life of the Buddha contained in chapter 14 of the *Mahāparinirvāna Sutra,* where Indra in the guise of one of the eight kinds of demons is said to have told the future Buddha the first two lines of a four-line verse and offered to supply the second two lines only if he would let himself be devoured. The man who in a later life was to become the Buddha was so determined to gain this teaching that he agreed to the demon's proposal.

The Master replied, "What's the price of rice in Xiang-zhou?"[1]

118

Someone asked Master Yunmen, "What was it like when the two worthies[2] met each other?"

The Master said, "That was no chance event."

119

Master Yunmen entered the Dharma Hall and said,

"Indra[3] and old Shakyamuni are having a fight about Buddhism in the monastery courtyard; it's quite a hubbub!"

With this the Master left his seat.[4]

120

"What is the actual point [the Sixth Patriarch of] Caoqi is driving at?"

The Master said, "I like to be outraged. I don't like to be pleased."

---

[1] Present-day Xiangfan city in the northern part of Hubei province. This important market town in the middle region of the Yangtze plain may have been the hometown of the questioner. Since rice was the most basic food, one must assume that everyone including the questioner knew its price. Yunmen may here question the kind of "confusion" that occupies the monk.

[2] The meeting between Vimalakīrti and Mañjushrī that is described in the *Vimalakīrti Sutra*.

[3] See section 158, note 3.

[4] Professor Iriya suggests that Yunmen is here instigating his disciples to take part in the fight in order to reconcile the two or to become the rejoicing third person.

"Why is that so?"

"If one encounters a swordsman on the road, one ought to offer him a sword; and to someone who is not a poet one doesn't present a poem."[1]

551c20–22

121

In the Dharma Hall for a public instruction, Yunmen said, "Fellow monks, you ought to grasp what it is that constitutes a patch-robed monk. Well, what is it that makes a patch-robed monk?"

[No answer.]

He added, "Great Perfection of Wisdom! Today we have great communal labor."

And he stepped down from his seat.

551c22–25

122

Someone asked Yunmen, "What was the purpose in [Bodhidharma's] coming from the West?"

The Master said, "The mountains, the rivers, the earth."[2]

The monk insisted, "Is there something beyond that?"

---

[1] It is possible to take this as "Answering you would be playing the harp for an ox," but I favor "If you meet a Zen-man, provoke him with an outrageous Zen-question!"

[2] It appears that the objects mentioned in this expression are representative of all phenomena that one is facing. The connection between the seer and the seen, the hearer and the heard, the subject and its objects, is a constant theme in Chan literature; thus it is for instance said that "[concerns arise] because outside you see mountains, rivers, and the earth" (case 25 of the *Blue Cliff Record,* T48: 166a19), or: "Baizhang said, 'All words, mountains, rivers, the earth: they all come back to one's self'" (ibid., case 2, 142b26), or "If there is a single thing in your breast, then mountains, rivers, and the earth appear in profusion before you; if there is not a single thing in your breast, then outside there is not so much as a tiny hair" (ibid., case 60, 192b19–20). See also section 80.

The Master said, "There is."

The questioner continued, "What is it?"

The Master said, "Old Shakyamuni is staying in India, and Bodhisattva Mañjushrī resides in China."

123

A monk asked, "What is it like when both father and mother are deceased?"

The Master replied, "Let's leave 'both are deceased' aside: who are your father and mother?"

The monk said, "The pain is deep."

The Master said, "I see, I see!"[1]

124

Someone asked Yunmen, "If a totally ignorant one comes: how do you help him?"

The Master replied, "Both cases[2] [his and yours] are taken care of by a single indictment."[3]

---

[1] If "father" and "mother" are not used allegorically here, Yunmen's reaction appears to be a compassionate one, although one cannot exclude irony even here. Cf. the fierce attack of Baizhang on a monk in similar circumstances (*Collection from the Founder's Halls,* 4.55, 13–14):

> A monk came crying into the Dharma Hall and Master [Baizhang] asked, "What's the matter, what's the matter?" The monk replied, "My father and mother both died! Please, Master, choose a day [for the funeral]." The Master cried, "Get out and come back tomorrow, I'll bury you together with them!"

[2] *Gongan* (Jap. kōan): see also section 46, p. 107, note 4, on *xianzheng gongan* for the legal context of early occurrences of this term, which acquired much prominence in later times. This exchange illustrates well how this term was used before it became famous.

[3] Yunmen's teacher Muzhou used to say that the case against someone was made as soon as he entered and before he even opened his mouth (see section 46).

551c29–
552a1

125

A monk asked Master Yunmen, "For whose benefit is it that you are teaching?"

The Master said, "Come closer and ask louder!"

The monk stepped forward and asked [once more].

The Master hit him.

552a1–3

126

Someone asked Master Yunmen, "How old are you, Master?"

The Master replied, "Seven times nine is sixty-eight."

The questioner asked, "Why would seven times nine be sixty-eight?"

The Master said, "I subtracted five years for you."[1]

552a4–25

127

Having entered the Dharma Hall for a formal instruction, Master Yunmen said:

"Reverend monks! Though you say 'What is the matter?'[2] you're still putting a head on top of a head[3] and frost on top of snow, you're blinking an eye in the coffin and are burning moxa

---

[1] This is not a mistranslation.

[2] Here, the answer "nothing whatsoever is the matter" is implied. It is thus a statement one would expect from a person for whom everything is fine, i.e., an enlightened one.

[3] See also the *Record of Linji,* T47 (500c4–6; Sasaki translation, p. 25):
I say to you that there is no Buddha, no Dharma, nothing to practice, nothing to prove. Just what are you seeking thus in the highways and byways? Blind men! You're putting a head on top of the one you already have. What do you yourself lack?

on a moxa burn scar.[1] This is quite a messy scene! But what can one do about it?

"Every one of you must strive for himself to obtain [a better] rebirth. Don't futilely tramp around China's districts and provinces! You just want to get hold of some trivial words and are waiting for some master's mouth to move; then you ask about Chan and the Dao, 'upward' and 'downward,' 'what is . . .' and 'what if . . . ,' and you stuff what you note down on big rolls of copying paper right into the bags of skin [that you are]. Wherever you go you gather in small groups around the fireplace, and many voices murmur in speculation: 'These are impartial and eloquent words and those are words conceived on the spot; these are words based on events and those are words that embody—embody the master or mistress in your house.' And once you've gobbled these words down you do nothing but talk in your sleep, saying, 'I have understood the Buddha Dharma.' It's quite obvious that by such pilgrimages you'll never ever[2] attain rest![3]

"And then there's the bunch who, as soon as they hear some talk about rest, shut their eyes while in hell.[4] They spend their life in a rat hole, sit under a dark mountain where ghosts roam, and say, 'I found a way in.' Do they see it even in a dream? What crime would it be to beat ten thousand people of this kind to death? This is called 'right from the outset no chance

---

[1] Actions that make no sense and are utterly superfluous.

[2] Literally, "in the year of the donkey." Because the donkey is not one of the animals in the Chinese twelve-year cycle, this simply means "never."

[3] Of course, "rest" here has a strong spiritual connotation (peace of mind, awakening).

[4] A metaphor for one's existential ostrich-policy: to close one's eyes to anxiety and unrest and pretend that one is at rest.

to meet an accomplished one.' After all, these are just windbags.

"If there really is something you see: come and show it to me, I'll discuss it with you! Don't vainly overlook that you don't know good from bad, and don't hold those senseless gatherings to get caught up in words! Don't let me see you [doing this], since if I caught you and found out about the wrong you did, I'd have to beat you up and cut you in half.[1] Don't you ever say that I didn't tell you!

"Is there any blood under your skin? What good is it to willfully victimize yourself wherever you go? Bunch of exterminators of Buddhism! You're no more than a pack of wild foxes! What are you all here for?"

And Master Yunmen at once chased the monks with his staff out of the Dharma Hall.

552a25–27

128

Someone asked, "The Honored Ones[2] of the ten directions all had a single gateway to ultimate liberation. What is this gateway?"

The Master said, "I can't tell."

The questioner went on, "Master, why can't you tell?"

The Master replied, "If you, just you, present the problem then I can."[3]

---

[1] A legal term that means "to cut off at the hip." This was a punishment for criminals.

[2] One of the ten epithets of an awakened one (buddha); Sanskrit *bhagavat*.

[3] This conversation is similar to the legendary story of Bodhidharma's meeting with the second patriarch, Shenguang Huike. The tradition has it that after having stood up to his hip in the snow and cut off his arm to show his determination to come to grips with his problem, Huike is finally allowed to tell Bodhidharma about his concern:

129

Someone asked Master Yunmen, "I request your instruction, Master!"

The Master said, "ABCDEF."

The questioner: "I don't understand."

The Master: "GHIJKL."[1]

130

Having entered the Dharma Hall for a formal instruction, Master Yunmen said:

"Your eyelashes stretch out horizontally in all ten directions, your eyebrows penetrate heaven and earth down to the yellow springs,[2] and Mt. Sumeru has blocked your throat. Now is there something [in what I said] that you understand? If you do: pick up Vietnam and smash it against Korea!"[3]

Huike: "Please, Master, bring peace into my heart-mind!" Bodhidharma: "Show me your heart-mind, and I will pacify it!" Huike: "I have searched for it, but I could not find it." Bodhidharma: "If you could search for it, how could it be your very own heart-mind? And how should I bring peace to it?" Then Bodhidharma said to Huike, "I have once and for all pacified the heart-mind for you. Do you now see it?" At these words, Huike was greatly awakened. (*Collection from the Founder's Halls*, 1.73, 6 ff)

[1] In the original, of course, the first Chinese characters a child had to learn to write are used.

[2] The underworld, the world of the dead.

[3] The almost identical talk in the second chapter of the *Record of Yunmen* (563c29–564a3) adds:

"In place [of his students, Master Yunmen] said: 'Ha!'"

552b15–16

131

Having entered the Dharma Hall for a formal instruction, Master Yunmen said:

"Get out, get out of here! You're fooling each other without end!"

Then Master Yunmen asked the assembly: "Is even to say what I just said a mistake?"

552b16–18

132

"What did the founder [Bodhidharma] intend when he came from the West?"

"You must not ask that!"[1]

"Yes."

"Bah! You don't even comprehend what I said!"

552b18–20

133

Someone asked, "When you make offerings to the arhats[2] today, do they come?"

Master Yunmen said, "If you don't ask, I won't answer."

"Please, Master, tell me!"

---

[1] Depending on where one puts the stress, this answer can have different meanings. Does Yunmen say that the questioner is not yet in a position to ask such a question (stress on *you*), or does he criticize the question as trite (stress on *that*), or does he imply that the questioner himself ought to answer that question (stress on *ask*)?

[2] Saints who are free from craving and rebirth and have thus reached the seventh stage of the bodhisattva path, where they are worthy of respect and offerings; or one of the ten epithets of a buddha. Even today, offerings to arhats are given during ceremonies on every first and fifteenth day in Sōtō Zen temples in Japan.

The Master said, "Fold hands in greeting in front of the main temple gate, and offer incense in the Buddha Hall."[1]

134

552b20–22

Someone asked Master Yunmen, "What is the patch-robed monk's very own matter?"

The Master said, "In the South, there's Master Xuefeng; in the North, there's Master Zhaozhou."[2]

The questioner continued, "Please, Master, don't complicate things!"

The Master said, "You must not dodge your question!"

The student said, "Yes."

The Master hit him.

135

552b25–c8

Having entered the Dharma Hall for a formal instruction, Master Yunmen said:

"Well, what has since ancient times been the matter? Right now I cannot help saying to all of you: What thing is there in the whole universe that is an object for you or stands in relation to you? If there is the slightest thing that forms an obstacle or constriction for you, come get hold of it for me! What is it that you call 'buddha' and 'patriarch'? What is it that you call mountain, river, the earth, sun, moon, and stars? And what

---

[1] This appears to be a standing expression used by teachers to effectively end the interview. It is likely that it involves a critical element, not unlike modern Japanese Rinzai masters' ringing of the bell during individual interviews: Get out of here!

[2] See section 86.

do you regard as the four elements[1] and the five components?[2]

"When I talk this way, I call it 'talk by a granny from a three-house hamlet.'[3] If I'd happen to come across a real pilgrim and he'd hear me talk like this, he couldn't be reproached if he grabbed me by my leg and threw me down the steps.

"Nevertheless [I ask you]: for what reason is this so? Don't take advantage of your glib mouthpiece for haphazard talk in here. [To be able to freely talk] you must first *be* this kind of man! If all of a sudden the ground on which you stand gets examined by me, you will be cornered and get your legs broken; will there be anything wrong with that?

"This being understood: is there someone right now who would like to question me about the essence of our [Chan] tradition? Let me reply with one turn [of phrase] and then go wherever I like!"

Just when some monk was about to ask, the Master hit him with his staff full on the mouth. Then he left his seat.

552c10–12

136

Master Yunmen entered the Dharma Hall and said,

"I've got a phrase, but I wouldn't dare to hope that you'd understand it. But is there [at least] someone able to cite one?"

---

[1] Earth, water, fire, and wind. These are the elements from which all things were considered to be made.

[2] The five skandhas (components of human beings): 1. form, matter; 2. reception, feeling; 3. conception, perception; 4. volition, mental functioning; and 5. discrimination, consciousness (see Sasaki, *Recorded Sayings,* note 113, p. 76).

[3] The grandmother showers her children and grandchildren with love and kindness; in Chan texts, expressions like "grandmotherly kindness" or "compassionate like a grandmother's heart" abound. Compassion shown by a grandmother from a three-house hamlet may be even greater since she has so few persons to distribute it to.

After a long silence he said, "I always thought that [only this] barbarian's beard was red, but it turns out that there are more red-bearded barbarians!'

Therewith the Master left his seat.

137

552c13–17

Having entered the Dharma Hall for a formal instruction, Master Yunmen said:

"I cannot help giving medicine to the dead horse. I'm telling you: 'What is it?[1] Is it east or west, north or south, being or non-being, seeing or hearing, up there beyond or down here below, so or not-so?'

"This is called 'boondock granny talk.'[2] But how many of you have reached this realm? Whether you're in accordance with it or not: may it come about at a quiet place!"[3]

With this the Master left the hall.

138

552c18–22

Having entered the Dharma Hall for a formal instruction, Master Yunmen said:

"Old monks everywhere say, 'You must realize that single thing without sound or form.' With words of this kind they fool people's children. Inside their tiny temples they are deluding themselves; not even in a dream have they ever seen the signifi-

---

[1] This question, whose subject matter is what Zen is about, was a favorite one of Yunmen's teacher Xuefeng.

[2] See also section 135, and note 3 of section 142.

[3] This magic formula was used at the end of magic incantations in Mahayana Buddhism. It could here be used like "Su-lu, su-lu" (see section 77)—i.e., as a means to drive off evil spirits and influences.

cance of our original teacher's tradition! For what purpose do they consume the alms of the faithful? When their time is up, every one of them will have to reimburse those almsgivers, panic as he may!

"Just you, each and every one of you, must make the effort by yourselves! Take care!"

552c27–29

139

Someone asked, "What is the pure immaculate Dharma body?"[1]

Master Yunmen replied, "That peony hedge!"

The monk asked, "Is it all right if I understand it in this way?"

The Master said, "A golden-haired lion!"[2]

553a1–2

140

Yunmen went up to the Dharma Hall, and on hearing the sound of the bell, he said,

---

[1] This expression is most often used in conjunction with the Vairocana Buddha (the great sunlight Buddha), who is a representation of the Dharma body. It symbolizes the pure reality of awakened buddhahood, which is free of the defilements of illusion. This buddhahood is not something far away; rather, it is in Chan viewed as the very nature of each person. Thus it is said in the *Record of Linji* (T47: 497b17) that "the threefold body is nothing other than the listener standing in front of me." So this question, while conjuring up the colorful image of Vairocana Buddha (which may be reflected in Yunmen's answer), appears to be about the questioner's own awakened, undefiled nature.

[2] This answer is quite a riddle, and various interpretations have been advanced: that the immobile lion with its potential violent moves stands in contrast to a peony hedge, or that the golden lion symbolizes the interpenetration of the universal and the particular. It seems possible to me that Yunmen, in effect, is giving a negative answer to the monk's question whether it was all right to simply accept this answer; thus I tend to read Yunmen's answer as: "[No, it's not all right. The body of immaculate reality is] a golden-haired lion!"

"The world is so wide and vast; why should I wear the seven-strip robe[1] at the sound of the bell?"

141

Having entered the Dharma Hall for a formal instruction, the Master said:

"One ought not to put frost on top of snow! Take care!"

With this the Master left the teacher's seat.

142

Having entered the Dharma Hall for a formal instruction, the Master said:

"These old shavepates everywhere! Sitting on round chairs[2] and long [meditation] benches, they want to acquire fame and profit. Asked about Buddha, they answer 'Buddha,' and asked about patriarch they answer 'patriarch,' and they shit and piss. [What they say] is just like information passed around among boondock grannies.[3] They don't even know good from bad!

"You're all just like them; [you ought to] have trouble to consume even water [with a good conscience]."[4]

---

[1] The outer robe. This is one of the three robes of a Buddhist monk. It is so called because it is made of seven strips of cloth. The nine-strip robe is the most gorgeous one, the five-strip robe the simplest. The seven-strip robe was apparently worn when attending formal talks of a master.

[2] A chair with round arm- and backrests used by Chan masters while giving formal talks, etc.

[3] Most commentators point out that this expression refers either simply to the passing on of information inside a village or to a game similar to "telephone," where each person has to whisper the words he has just heard into his neighbor's ear.

[4] **Yunmen seems** to imply that these monks are so utterly worthless creatures

553a8–9

143

Having entered the Dharma Hall for a formal instruction, the Master said:

"Every person originally has the radiant light[1]—yet when it is looked at, it is not seen: dark and obscure!"

With this the Master left the teacher's seat.

553a13–28

144

Having entered the Dharma Hall for a formal instruction, the Master said:

"All of you who come and go for no reason: What are you looking for in [this monastery] here? I only know how to eat and drink and shit. What else would I be good for?

"You're making pilgrimages all over the place, studying Chan and asking about the Dao. Let me ask you: What have you managed to learn in all those places? Try presenting that!"

Again, he said: "In the meantime, you cheat the Master in your own house. Is that all right? When you manage to find a little slime on my ass, you lick it off, take it to be your own self, and say: 'I understand Chan, I understand the Dao!' Even if you manage to read the whole Buddhist canon—so what?!

"The old masters couldn't help it. When they saw you run about aimlessly, they said to you 'supreme wisdom (bodhi) and nirvana.' They really buried you; they drove in a stake and tied you to it.[2] Again, when they saw that you didn't understand,

---

that they don't even merit receiving and consuming water, a natural resource available to everyone.

[1] This is a metaphor for awakened wisdom that breaks the darkness of delusion.

[2] See the *Record of Linji* (T47: 497c11): "Bodhi and nirvana are like hitching posts for asses."

they said to you: 'It's not bodhi and nirvana.' Knowing this sort of thing already shows that you're down on your luck; [but to make matters worse,] you're looking for comments and explanations by others. You exterminators of Buddhism, you've been like this all along! And where has this brought you today?

"When I was on pilgrimage some time ago, there was a bunch of people who gave me explanations. They didn't have bad intentions, but one day I saw through them [and realized] that they are laughingstocks. If I don't die in the next four or five years, I'll get these exterminators of Buddhism and break their legs!

"These days there are plenty of temple priests everywhere who fake it: why don't you go and join them? What dry piece of shit are you looking for in here?"

The Master stepped down from his seat, and he hit and chased the monks out of the hall with his staff.

Essential Sayings from the
Master's Room

■ ■ ■

553c25–27

145

Instructing the assembly, the Master said:

"Heaven, earth, and the whole world in all ten directions are shattered to pieces by one blow of my staff.

"If you abandon the entirety of the written Buddhist teachings[1] as well as Bodhidharma's coming from the West, it won't do. Yet if you hold on to them, you won't be worth a shout."[2]

554a1–3

146

Instructing the assembly, the Master said:

"The twenty-eight Indian and six Chinese founders[3] as well as the whole empire's teachers are all on the tip of this staff.

---

[1] Literally: the twelve divisions of teachings of the three vehicles.

[2] The shout is one of the frequently used teaching devices of Chan masters (see also section 94); here it may stand for other devices as well or even for the teaching activity of the masters in general. The next section has a similar theme.

[3] This is the legendary lineage linking the historical Buddha with the Chan tradition. For the Indian part, see the tentative Sanskrit reconstruction of the

"But even if you'd manage to understand and discern this quite clearly, you'd still be but halfway there. As long as you don't let go, you're nothing but a wild fox ghost!"

147

One day the Master said:

"Because of their compassion, all the venerables since olden days held conversations that fell into the weeds;[1] through their words you will know what they are about. You would not be in that position had they [only] held talks that left the weeds.[2] So there are collected and condensed anecdotes. Haven't you read the following story:

> Reverend Yangshan asked a monk, "Where have you just come from?"
>
> "From the Lu mountains," replied the monk.
>
> Yangshan said, "In that case, did you visit the Five Elders Peak?"
>
> "I've never been there," answered the monk.

---

names of the twenty-eight Indian founders by Professor Gishin Tokiwa reproduced with some questionable changes in Appendix G of Hisao Inagaki's *Glossary of Zen Terms* (Kyoto: Nagata Bunshōdō, 1991). The traditional six founders (patriarchs) of Chinese Zen are Bodhidharma, Huike, Sengcan, Daoxin, Hongren, and Huineng.

[1] "Falling into the weeds" is a vernacular expression referring to a teacher who lowers himself compassionately into the weeds of delusion and ignorance. In this sense it corresponds to a "downward" activity—i.e., an activity that enters into the contradictions and delusions of the world in order to lead people beyond that ("upward").

[2] Straight talk by the awakened that does not make any concessions to the illusions (weeds) of the audience; in contrast to talk that is adapted to the circumstances and compassionately "enters the weeds."

Yangshan rejoined, "You've never even been to the mountain!"

Master Yunmen said: "These words are all [examples of] having conversations in the weeds out of compassion."

554a10–12

148

The Master once said:

"If you say 'this very mind is buddha,'[1] you provisionally accept the slave as master and life-and-death (samsara) as nirvana. This is precisely like cutting off one's head in pursuit of life. Talking about buddhas and founders and their respective intentions is just like snatching away your own eyeballs while looking for soap berries."[2]

554a13–15

149

Master Yunmen cited:

A man of old has said: "[Xiangyan] awakened to the Dao upon hearing a sound, and [Master Lingyun] got enlightened upon seeing a color."[3]

Master Yunmen said: "How about 'awakening to the Dao upon hearing a sound' and 'getting enlightened upon seeing a color'?"

---

[1] This is a famous saying in the Chan tradition; it is usually attributed to Master Mazu.

[2] See section 179 for a variation on this theme.

[3] These are references to Master Xiangyan Zhixian (died 898), a disciple of Baizhang who was enlightened while sweeping when a piece of rock struck a bamboo, and to Master Lingyun Zhiqin, who also lived in the Tang era and awakened to the Dao when seeing a peach blossom.

Then he said: "The Bodhisattva Guanyin[1] is taking a coin and is coming to buy a sesame flatcake."

Lowering his hand, he added: "I see! It's just a dumpling!"[2]

150

554a16–20

The Master once said:

"The lantern is your self. Yet when you hold your bowl and eat your food, the food is not your self."

A monk asked: "How about when the food is my self?"

The Master cried: "You wild fox ghost! Country bumpkin!"[3]

He added: "Come, come! Isn't it you who said that the food is your self?"

The monk said, "Yes."

The Master exclaimed: "In the year of the donkey you'll see it in a dream, you hick!"

---

[1] Guanyin (Sanskrit Avalokiteshvara, Jap. Kannon), a bodhisattva known for boundless compassion. Professor Iriya suggests that the literal meaning of the Chinese name Guanyin ("seeing sounds") could play a role here: his sight is supposed to be so good that he even sees sounds.

[2] A steam-cooked rice-flour dumpling, usually of round dome-shape with some filling. Does Yunmen here make fun of Guanyin, who is supposed to see even sounds yet cannot even distinguish a flatcake from a dome-shaped dumpling? Professor Iriya feels that Yunmen may here have taken over the role of Guanyin, gratefully holding up an imaginary cake and then lowering his hands to discover with astonishment that he did not get what he wanted—which might also be a criticism of the audience that could not produce what Guanyin was after, on the line of: "I threw in a hook to catch a giant fish—but what did I manage to catch? A frog!" (section 109).

[3] By such provocations Yunmen sought to test people who by their words or actions suggested having broken through duality (here: the duality of food and self).

554a21–23

151

The Master once said: "True emptiness does not destroy being, and true emptiness does not differ from form."

Then a monk asked: "What is true emptiness?"

The Master answered: "Do you hear the sound of the bell?"

The monk replied: "That's the sound of the bell."

The Master cried: "Will you see it in a dream in the year of the donkey?"

554b8–13

152

Master Yunmen quoted a verse by Sanping:[1]

This very seeing and hearing is not seeing and hearing.[2]

Master Yunmen said: "What do you call seeing and hearing?"

[Continuing the quotation, he said,]

There's no further sound or shape that could reveal itself to you.

The Master said: "Does anyone want to stick his oar in?"
[He continued quoting,]

If you realize this right here, then nothing will be the matter.

---

[1] Sanping Yizhong lived from 781 to 872.

[2] The *Collection from the Founder's Halls,* 2.29, 5 ff., quotes two more verses by Sanping, which begin with "What is perceived is originally not soiled" and "What is perceived is originally not caused." See Seizan Yanagida, *Zen no Bunka (Shiryōhen): Zenrinsōbōden,* vol. 1 (Kyoto: Kyoto daigaku jinbun kagaku kenkyūjo, 1988), p. 244b. The same three verses appear also in the *Record of the Mirror of the Teachings* (Zongjinglu, T48: 944b1 ff.).

The Master said: "Is anything the matter?"
[He finished the quotation,]

And essence and function[1] hinder neither distinction nor non-distinction.

The Master said, "Word is essence, essence is word."
Again, he lifted his staff and remarked, "This staff is essence, and the lantern is function. It's distinguishing without distinguishing. Haven't you read the statement 'All knowledge is pure'?"[2]

153

554b16–19

The Master told the following story:

> A monk said to Master Zhaozhou, "I have just joined the monastery and am asking for your teaching." Zhaozhou asked back, "Have you already eaten your gruel?" The monk replied, "Yes." Zhaozhou said: "Go wash your bowl!"[3]

Master Yunmen said: "Well, tell me: was what Zhaozhou said a teaching or not? If you say that it was: what is it that Zhaozhou told the monk? If you say that it wasn't: why did the monk in question attain awakening?"

---

[1] Essence *(ti)* and function *(yong)* are two concepts that play an exceedingly important role in Chinese philosophy, especially in Buddhist and Neo-Confucian thought. Together, essence and function characterize an entity.

[2] See section 17.

[3] In the *Record of Zhaozhou* (ZZ119: 161a18–b1) the initial question by the monk is different: "What is my self?"

554b20–21

154

Master Yunmen mentioned the following story:

> A monk asked Xuefeng for instruction. Xuefeng said to him: "What is it?"[1] At these words the monk attained great awakening.

Master Yunmen said: "What is it that Xuefeng had told him?"

554c12–14

155

Master Yunmen mentioned the following words by Panshan:[2]

> When both the light and the [illuminated] objects are forgotten: what is that?[3]

Master Yunmen said: "Even though he speaks like this, he's still only at the halfway stage. This is not yet the way of breakthrough."

A monk then asked: "What is the way of breakthrough?"

---

[1] See section 137, note 1.

[2] Panshan Baoji (dates unknown) was a successor of Mazu. The fragment cited by Yunmen stems from a statement by Panshan that reads as follows:
> As to the moon of the mind: it is lone and perfect, and its light engulfs the myriad phenomena. If its light does not shine on objects, the objects have no existence either. When both light and objects are forgotten: what is that? (*Record of the Transmission of the Lamp,* T51: 253b15–17).

[3] The interdependence of the human mind and its objects is the core of the "Consciousness Only" or "Representation Only" movement of Buddhism and also forms a cornerstone of many philosophical works by European thinkers (for instance, Kant's *Critique of Pure Reason* and Schopenhauer's *On the Fourfold Root of the Principle of Sufficient Reason*).

Master Yunmen said: "The Flower Peak of Tiantai, the stone bridge of Zhaozhou."[1]

156

554c20–22

Master Yunmen mentioned the following story:

> Xuefeng told a monk: "Come closer!" When the monk did as told, Xuefeng said: "Get out!"

After telling this story, Master Yunmen asked a monk: "How can you utter a phrase of greeting with hands folded at your chest?[2] If you can say such a phrase, you'll meet Xuefeng!"

157

554c23–24

Master Yunmen quoted a saying by the Third Patriarch:

> When mind does not arise, the myriad things have no fault.[3]

Master Yunmen said: "That's all he understood!"
Then he raised his staff and added: "Is anything amiss in the whole universe?"

---

[1] These are two proverbial sights. As touched upon in note 2 on p. 111 (section 52), we find here first a critique of the negative expression by Panshan and then a positive expression. It is possible that the specific objects are not of great significance in this context; Yunmen could, as he often did, also have adduced a lantern, a pillar, a mountain, or something else.

[2] Folding one's hands at one's chest is a Chinese gesture of respectful greeting that is not limited to Buddhist circles.

[3] This is a quotation from the *Inscription on Trusting in Mind* (T51: 457a18).

555a3–7

158

Master Yunmen mentioned the following story:

> A monk asked Master Ganfeng:[1] "[It is said:] 'The Honored Ones of the ten directions all had a single gateway to ultimate liberation.'[2] I wonder where that gateway is!"
>
> Ganfeng drew a line with his staff and said: "In here!"

Master Yunmen held up his fan and said, "When this fan jumps to the uppermost heaven, it strikes the nose of Indra,[3] and when it gives a blow to the carp of the Eastern Sea, the rain pours down in torrents! Do you understand?"[4]

555a16–21

159

Master Yunmen related the following story:

> Yangshan asked a monk: "Where have you last been?" The monk replied: "In the south." Yangshan took up his staff and said: "Did they talk there about this?" The monk answered: "They didn't." "If they didn't talk about this,

---

[1] Yuezhou Ganfeng (dates unknown) was a disciple of Dongshan Liangjie (807–869).

[2] See also section 128, where the same quotation is used in a question to the master.

[3] Originally a powerful Hindu deity, Indra was adopted by Buddhism as a protective deity of Buddhism and its followers. He was thought to reside in a palace in the highest heaven (the thirty-third) on Mt. Sumeru.

[4] This appears to be an antithesis to the rather static view of Ganfeng. Yunmen was fond of such very dynamic expressions; see also section 197, where Yunmen's staff turns into a dragon. Such statements are in Yunmen's characteristic manner formulated as challenges and thus fit DeMartino's definition of the koan (see page 53).

did they talk about that?" The monk said: "They didn't."
Yangshan directed the monk to go and take his place in the
hall, and the monk did as told. Yangshan called him once
more. The monk answered, "Yes?" Yangshan said:
"Come closer." The monk went closer. Yangshan then
struck him.

Master Yunmen said: "If Yangshan hadn't said those last
words, how could he have discerned that man?"

160

Master Yunmen told the following story:

> Xuefeng said to a monk: "Come here!" When the monk
> did as told, Xuefeng said: "Where are you going?" "I'm
> going to group work," the monk answered. Xuefeng said:
> "Go!"

Master Yunmen remarked: "This is an example of 'knowing a man through his words.'"

161

Master Yunmen mentioned the following episode:

> Jiashan was sitting when Dongshan[1] arrived and said:
> "How are you doing?" Jiashan replied: "Just so."

Master Yunmen said in place of Dongshan: "What will
you do if I won't go along with that?"
In place of Jiashan, Yunmen gave a shout.

---

[1] Jiashan Shanhui (805–881) and Dongshan Liangjie (807–869). The latter is
one of the two men who later was termed a founder of the Caodong/Sōtō
lineage of Zen.

Again, Master Yunmen brought up Jiashan's words "Just so"[1] and said: "I see, you're just in a frog's hole!"

Then he added: " 'Just so'—yet it's hard to attain."[2]

162

Master Yunmen cited the verse of a founder:[3]

> Each separate entity (dharma) is what the Buddhist teaching (Dharma) is originally about.

Master Yunmen said: "Walking, standing, sitting, and reclining are not what the Buddhist teaching is originally about. Nothing whatsoever—be it mountains or rivers or the earth or your dressing and eating day and night—is what the Buddhist teaching is originally about. What's wrong with that?"[4]

Again, Master Yunmen cited:

> The teaching (Dharma) is at root a teaching without object (dharma).[5]

---

[1] See also section 196, note 1.

[2] This is a classical example of the manner in which Yunmen not only presents a koan to his disciples but on top of that puts it into question. He thus doubles the challenge.

[3] This is a verse attributed to the first Indian patriarch, Mahakashapa. A tentative translation of the whole poem (*Record of the Transmission of the Lamp*, T51: 206b3–4) reads as follows:
> *Each dharma is what the Dharma is originally about:*
> *neither teaching nor no-teaching.*
> *But how can there be in a teaching*
> *both teaching and no-teaching?*

[4] In other words: it is okay if a staff is just a staff.

[5] This is a quotation from a poem ascribed to the Buddha (T51: 205c1–2), which is the point of reference of Mahakashapa's verse. Tentative translation:

The Master held up his staff and said: "This isn't 'at root without object.' "

163

555b14–17

Master Yunmen cited the words of Mr. Bao:[1]

> Just as my "I" is empty, all separate entities (dharmas) are empty. This applies to all there is, regardless of its kind.

Master Yunmen said: "[Yet] when you stand you're not aware of standing, and when you walk you're not aware of walking; and the four major elements [which constitute the physical universe] and the five components [of living beings] cannot be grasped. Come on, where do you see the mountains and rivers and the earth? You, just you who every day take your bowl and eat rice: what do you call 'rice'? Where is there a single grain of rice?!"

164

555b18–20

Master Yunmen quoted:

> All sounds are the Buddha's voice; all shapes are the Buddha's form.

The Master picked up the fly-whisk and said: "What is this? If you say it is a fly-whisk, you won't even understand the Chan of a granny from a three-house hick town."

The teaching (Dharma) is at root a teaching without object (dharma)
but the objectless teaching is nevertheless a teaching.
How could each thing be the teaching
if you now were attached to no-teaching?

[1] This man is not otherwise known.

555b24–27

165

The Master once said: "Do you want to know the founding masters?" Pointing with his staff, he said: "They are jumping around on your heads! Do you want to know their eyeball?[1] It's right under your feet!"

He added: "This [kind of guidance] is offering tea and food to ghosts and spirits.[2] Nevertheless, these ghosts and spirits are not satisfied."

555b28–c2

166

The Master once said: "Talking to you about enlightened wisdom, final deliverance, thusness, and liberation means burning maple incense[3] and offering it to you. Talking to you about buddhas and founders means burning 'golden heat' incense and offering it to you. Talking to you about transcending the buddhas and going beyond the founders means burning bottled incense and offering it to you. Take refuge in the Buddha, his teaching, and the monastic community!"

With this he left the Dharma Hall.

---

[1] The "eyeball of the founding masters" stands for their awakening—i.e., their realization of the core ("eye") of Buddhist teaching. In the Chan tradition, this teaching is often called the "treasury of the eye of the genuine teaching" (Jap. *shōbōgenzō*), which is also the title of the major work of Dōgen Kigen (1200–1252), the father of Japanese Sōtō Zen. See also section 14, note 2.

[2] In one of his talks, Deshan compares the crowds of monks who run around and proclaim to be Chan masters to such "ghosts and spirits" (Dahui's *Treasury of the Eye of the Genuine Teaching* [Zhengfayanzang], ZZ118: 19a5).

[3] This incense is made from the resin of the Chinese maple tree. It is not of high quality, and the two other kinds mentioned (golden heat incense and bottled incense) are even cheaper forms of "instant" incense. Yunmen appears to compare this kind of talk to a cheap offering to his audience.

167

555c3–6

The Master one day held up his staff and mentioned a teaching that goes:

> The ordinary person in all sincerity says that this [staff] exists, [representatives of] the two vehicles[1] of Buddhist teaching explain that it doesn't exist, the pratyeka buddhas say it exists as an illusion, and the bodhisattvas empty it as it is.

Then Master Yunmen said: "When a patch-robed monk sees this staff, he just calls it a staff; when he walks, he just walks; and when he sits, he just sits. In all of this he cannot be stirred."[2]

168

555c12–14

Once, when the Master had finished drinking tea, he held up the cup and said: "All the buddhas of the three periods[3] have finished listening to the teaching; they have pierced the bottom of this cup and are going away. Do you see? Do you see? If you don't understand, look it up in an encyclopedia!"

169

555c15–20

Master Yunmen cited Panshan's[4] words:

---

[1] The small vehicle (Hinayana or Theravada) and the great vehicle (Mahayana).

[2] See section 171 for a description of persons who are still unable to simply walk when walking, etc.

[3] The awakened ones of the past, present, and future.

[4] Panshan Baoji. See section 155, note 2.

When the light [of the knowing subject] is not one that confronts objects[1] and the objects are not existent things either: when both subject and object are forgotten, what further thing is there?

Master Yunmen said: "If the whole world is the light [of the subject]: what are you calling your 'self'? But even if you had managed to know that light, the objects would still be out of your reach. What shitty light and objects are there? And if neither subject nor object can be grasped: what else is there?"

He added: "These are collected and condensed anecdotes uttered out of compassion by the men of old. Realize [what they are about] right here with the utmost clarity! It won't do if you let go. Yet if you don't let go . . . !!"

Then the Master raised his hands and said: "Su-lu! Su-lu!"[2]

555c21–24

170

Master Yunmen quoted the words of Fu Dashi:[3]

The river of meditation follows the currents yet is calm;
the waters of samadhi go along with the waves yet are limpid.

---

[1] The translation "objects" is chosen in this context because there is an opposition of the light that stands for the subject or subjective mind and that which it confronts. Cf. also Huangbo's *Essentials of the Method of Transmitting Mind* (Ch. Chuanxin fayao, Jap. Denshin hōyō), which says (T48 381a20):
The ordinary man holds on to objects *(jing),* the man of the Way holds on to mind. When mind and objects are both forgotten: that is the true Dharma.

[2] See section 77, p. 124, note 1. It is conceivable that the master uttered this spell as a kind of purification after having said too much.

[3] Fu Dashi (497–569) was a famous Chinese layman of the Six Dynasties period, noted for his efforts to alleviate the sufferings of the people and to spread Buddhism. He was sometimes called the Chinese Vimalakīrti.

The Master seized his staff, pointed at the lantern, saying: "Well, do you see it? If you say that you see it, you're an ordinary Joe. If you say that you don't see it: you've got a pair of eyes, haven't you? How do you understand this?"

After a long pause he again took his staff and said: "The whole world is not a wave!"

171

555c24–28

Master Yunmen once seized his staff, banged it on the seat and said,

"All sounds are the Buddha's voice, and all forms are the Buddha's shape. Yet when you hold your bowl and eat your food, you hold a 'bowl-view'; when you walk, you hold a 'walk-view'; and when you sit you have a 'sit-view.' The whole bunch of you behaves this way!"[1]

The Master took his staff and drove them all away at once.

172

556a7–9

Master Yunmen cited the words of the Overnight Enlightened One[2]:

The spiritual action of the six senses is empty without being empty; the perfect shine of the singular [mani jewel] is formless form.[3]

---

[1] See the end of section 167 for a description of an accomplished monk.

[2] This is Yongjia Xuanjue, who is said to have received the Sixth Patriarch's transmission after one night's stay at the patriarch's temple.

[3] This quotation stems from *Yongjia's Song on Realizing the Way* (T48: 395c21). See also the *Record of Linji* (T47: 497b13):

What is lacking among our manifold activities today? The spiritual light emanating from your six senses never ceases to shine.

The Master held up his fly-whisk and said, "This is the perfect light, it is formless form. What do you call form? Come on, try taking that up with me!"

556a15–16

173

Citing the *Wisdom Sutra,* Yunmen said,

> [Oh purity of all-encompassing wisdom,] non-dual, undi-vided, without difference, not separate . . .[1]

He pointed to a pillar and said, "How much has this to do with the *Wisdom Sutra?*"

556a17–19

174

The Master cited a scripture that says,

> The sutras and magic spells, indeed all letters and words, are not at all in conflict with the true form.

Yunmen held up his staff and asked, "What is this? If you say it is a staff, you go to hell. If it isn't a staff, what is it?"

556a24–26

175

The Master once said, "[Actions of Chan masters such as] snapping fingers, chuckling, raising eyebrows, winking eyes, picking up a mallet, holding up a whisk, and sometimes [drawing] a circle: these are nothing but people-catchers.[2] What one calls Buddha Dharma has never yet been expressed in words. If it had,

---

[1] See section 79.

[2] These are long poles with attached hooks that allow catching dangerous criminals but were also used by firefighters to save trapped people.

that would have been no more than dropping shit and spraying piss."[1]

176

556b8–12

At a donated meal, the Master took one bite of a sesame bun and said, "I bit Indra's[2] nose. Indra is in agony!"

Then he pointed with his staff [to the monks' feet] and said: "He is right under your feet, transformed into old Shakyamuni! Do you see? Do you see?"

"The King of Hell, Yama,[3] hears my talk and is laughing out loud, saying: 'Ha ha, monk, you're quite up to it, I can't do a thing with you! But if someone's not up to it, he's completely in my hands!' "

177

556c5–8

Master Yunmen related the following conversation:

A monk asked Xuansha, "What is my self?"
Xuansha answered, "Just your self!"

Master Yunmen remarked, "Immeasurably great men have gotten caught up in the stream of words."

A monk asked Yunmen, "What is my self?"

The Master said, "[The one who,] when a man in the street invites you monks to a donated meal, is joining the queue to get some food!"

---

[1] See also the beginning of section 41.

[2] See section 158, p.164, note 3.

[3] See section 46, p. 108, note 1.

556c9–12

178

At a donated meal, the Master held up a sesame flatcake and said: "I offer food only to Southern Chinese people from Jiangxi and the regions east and west of the Zhe river.[1] I don't offer any food to people from the North."[2]

A monk asked, "Why do you only offer food to the people from Jiangxi and the regions east and west of the Zhe River but not to people from the North?"

The Master answered, "[Because in North China] the weather is cold and the days are short, and two people share one bowl."

556c29–
557a2

179

Master Yunmen cited the following story:

> Xuefeng said, "A man sitting next to a rice basket is starving to death, and a fellow by a river is dying of thirst."
>
> Xuansha commented, "A man sitting in a rice basket is starving to death, and a fellow up to his head in water is dying of thirst."

Master Yunmen said, "His whole body *is* rice, his whole body *is* water!"

557a17–20

180

Master Yunmen cited an ancient [poem]:

> In perfect tranquillity the form of emptiness is reflected.[3]

---

[1] This is the Zhejiang region south of Shanghai, where Yunmen was born.

[2] In section 198, Yunmen says just the opposite: "I don't offer any food to monks from the South. I offer it only to those from the North."

[3] This is part of the enlightenment poem of Master Danxia cited in *Collection from the Founder's Halls* (1.167, 2–5). The poem sings about suchness and the

The Master extended his hands and said, "Where can one attain the mountains, the rivers, the earth?"

He added,

All-embracing wisdom pervades and knows no hin-drance.[1]

Master Yunmen said, "The staff goes to India and comes back to Korea."

Then he hit the platform and said, "This is your nose!"

181

557a24–27

A monk asked, "What is my self?"

Master Yunmen said, "I, this old monk, enter mud and water."[2]

The monk exclaimed, "So I will crush my bones and tear my body to pieces!"[3]

The Master shouted and said, "The water of the whole great ocean is on your head.[4] Quickly, speak! Quickly, speak!"

The monk was left without words.

In his place, the Master said: "I know that you, Master, fear that I'm not quite genuine."

---

perfection of things as they are and ends with: "Heaven and earth are empty like a cave; in perfect tranquillity the form of emptiness is reflected, throwing brightness on the one way of suchness."

[1] See also section 111.

[2] This image is used for compassionate masters who spare no effort for the sake of their disciples.

[3] This stems from *Yongjia's Song on Realizing the Way* (T48: 396c21):
Crushing one's bones and tearing one's body to pieces is still not sufficient recompense [for the teacher's efforts on our behalf].

[4] The greatest imaginable pressure is on you. Or: I am already at the bottom of the sea.

557a28–b1

182

The Master once said: "Even if one may state that in the whole universe not the slightest thing is amiss, it is still but a turn of phrase. When you do not see uniformity, it can be called 'half the issue.'[1] But even if you're there, you must realize that there is a time when the whole is at stake."

557b4–7

183

Master Yunmen once said: "The manifold explanations about enlightened wisdom and final deliverance, about thusness and buddha-nature are all discussions that descend [into the realm of the conditioned]. Whether one picks up the mallet or raises the whisk, there will again be endless explanations. But such discussions amount to something all the same."

A monk asked: "Please, Master, say something beyond [the conditioned]!"

The Master replied, "You've all been standing for a long time. Quickly bow three times!"[2]

557b18–20

184

Master Yunmen mentioned three kinds of people: "The first gets awakened when hearing a talk, the second gets awakened when called, and the third turns round and leaves when hearing

---

[1] In perfect concentration (samadhi), uniformity can be "experienced"; but this kind of uniformity is again different from multiplicity or from non-concentrated states of mind, and thus there still is duality. The "whole" of which Yunmen speaks goes an all-important step further (see page 64).

[2] I.e., "That's it for today."

that anything is brought up. Tell me, what does turning around and going away mean?"

He added: "[The third] also deserves thirty blows!"

185

557b25–28

Master Yunmen quoted the words:

> I'll give you medicine according to your disease.[1] Well,
> the whole world is medicine plants; which one is your-
> self?[2]

Master Yunmen said, "One comes across a weed, and it turns out to be an orchid."

A monk said, "Please, Master, instruct me further."

The Master clapped his hands once, held up his staff, and said: "Take this staff!"

The monk took it and broke it in two.

The Master remarked, "Even so, you still deserve thirty blows."

186

557b29–c2

Master Yunmen mentioned the following story:

> At the end of the summer [training period] Cuiyan[3] said in
> a formal talk, "I have been talking to you monks through-

---

[1] This is an image frequently used in Chan literature. For example, Master Linji said, "Whatever I say, it is all temporary medicine in response to a disease" (*Record of Linji*, T47: 498b18). Later on, Linji says the same of all Buddhist teachings (502c8–9).

[2] I was unable to find these two sentences in texts other than the ones that simply replicate this whole conversation.

[3] Cuiyan Lingcan was a master in the Xuefeng tradition who lived during the Five Dynasties period (907–960).

out the summer; look whether I still have eyebrows or not!"

Baofu said, "Thieves have an uneasy heart."[1]

Changqing said, "They've grown!"[2]

Master Yunmen said, "Stuck!"

557c16–19

187

Master Yunmen quoted the *Heart Sutra,* which says:

There is neither eye nor ear nor nose nor tongue nor body nor mind.

The Master said, "Because you have eyes that see, you're unable to say that there is no eye. And since you're looking right now, you cannot say that there is no seeing.

"Even so, you see it all—and what's wrong with that? Yet nothing can be grasped. What sense-object is there?"

557c20–21

188

Master Yunmen cited:

The light [of the Buddha] serenely shines on worlds as numerous as the sand grains of the River Ganges.

He asked a monk, "Isn't this a verse by Chang Zhuo the Genius?"[3]

---

[1] A Chinese proverb signifying a bad conscience.

[2] The Chinese say that talking a lot makes one's eyebrows grow.

[3] This was a Five Dynasties and early Song layman whose precise dates are unknown; he studied under the masters Chanyue and Shishuang (see note 2, p. 179). The quotation is part of an enlightenment poem in eight verses that is featured in the *Compendium of the Five Lamps* (Wudeng huiyuan, ZZ138: 100a).

The monk replied, "It is."
Yunmen said, "Failed."[1]

189

558a1–4

Master Yunmen said,

> A monk asked Master Shishuang:[2] "Do the [written Buddhist] teachings contain what the [Chan] founders aimed at?" Master Shishuang replied, "Yes, they do."
>
> The monk went on asking, "And what is the Founder's aim that is contained in these teachings?" Master Shishuang replied, "Don't look for it inside the scrolls!"

Master Yunmen said in place of Shishuang, "Don't be ungrateful to me! Anyway, what good is it to sit in a trench full of shit?"

558a5–7

190

Master Yunmen cited [the following episode]:

> Master Chuyuan of Shishuang[3] said: "You must know that there is a phrase of special transmission outside the written tradition."

---

[1] "Failed" as used in a debate or an exam. Master Dahui said, "The moment you open your mouth, I know you've failed" (*Record of Dahui* [Dahui yulu], T47: 856a12).

[2] Shishuang Quingzhu (807–888). This master was famous for having practiced seated meditation for twenty years without lying down and for having refused to accept the honorary purple robe offered by a Tang emperor.

[3] See previous note.

A monk asked Shishuang: "What is this phrase of special transmission outside the written tradition?"

Master Shishuang replied: "A non-phrase."

Master Yunmen said: "A non-phrase is all the more a phrase!"

558a8–10

191

Master Yunmen mentioned the following episode:

Master Dongshan[1] said: "You must know that there is something which goes beyond 'Buddha.' "

A monk asked, "What is it that goes beyond Buddha?"

Master Dongshan replied: "Non-Buddha."

Master Yunmen commented: "He calls it 'non-' because he can neither name nor attain it!"

558a13–15

192

Master Yunmen mentioned the following:

[Pronouncements such as:] "The Purity of the Dharma body [is nothing other than] any sound and form" are without doubt very subtle statements.

[Master Yunmen asked:] "How about this 'purity,' without any subtleties?"

He added, "And how about the Dharma body?"

[When nobody answered] the Master said, "The six do not take it in."[2]

---

[1] See section 161, p. 166, note 1.

[2] The "six" are the traditional six "sense" organs (eyes, ears, nose, tongue, tactile body, and mind) or the six corresponding sense-objects and faculties.

He added: "The twenty-eight star formations of the thirty-third heaven."[1]

193

558a20–25

Once the Master said:

"As long as the light has not yet broken through,[2] there are two kinds of disease: 1. The first consists in seeing oneself facing objects and being left in the dark about everything.[3] 2. The second consists in having been able to pierce through to the emptiness of all separate entities (dharmas)—yet there still is something that in a hidden way is like an object.

"[Views about] the body of the teaching also exhibit two kinds of disease: 1. Having been able to reach the body of the Buddhist teaching, one still has subjective views and is at the margin of that teaching because one has not gotten rid of one's attachment to it. 2. Even though one has managed to penetrate through to the body of the Buddhist teaching, one is still unable to let go of it. But if one examines this [teaching] thoroughly, it's stone-dead. That's also a disease!"

None of these can offer any help in grasping the non-dual (and thus ungraspable) Dharma body. See case 47 of the *Blue Cliff Record*.

[1] Does Yunmen add this as a comment to his own answer ("Neither do the twenty-eight star formations of the thirty-third heaven") or as an answer to his question about the Dharma body?

[2] The light (*guang*) is commonly used in Chan texts as a metaphor for enlightenment. For example, Master Linji (*Record of Linji*, T47: 498b13) describes enlightenment as follows:

> Everywhere is purity, light penetrates all directions, and the myriad things are, as they are, one.

[3] Yunmen expressed his most pressing problem in similar terms when he went to see Master Muzhou: "The matter of my self is not clarified."

194

Master Yunmen mentioned the following episode:

> The Buddha asked an adherent of another religion: "What is in your view the essential?"

Master Yunmen answered in place of the adherent: "Hey, old monk, I've seen through you!"

> The other religion's adherent answered: "What I regard as essential is not to be taken in by anything."

Master Yunmen said in place of the Buddha: "Your turn!"[1]

> The Buddha said: "You *do* regard it as essential not to be taken in by anything, do you?"

Master Yunmen answered in place of the adherent: "Hey, Gautama, don't make [yourself] lose the [point of your] question!"

195

Master Yunmen cited Master Xuefeng's words:

> The whole world is you. Yet you keep thinking that there is something else . . .[2]

Master Yunmen said: "Haven't you read the *Shūrangama Sutra* which says, 'Sentient beings are all upside down;[3] they delude themselves and chase after things'?"

---

[1] Show me that you are not taken in by anything.

[2] This saying is found in the *Record of Xuefeng* (Xuefeng yulu, ZZ119: 476d14–15).

[3] In Buddhism, the term "upside down" is often used as the opposite of the true, awakened way of being and seeing—i.e., man's state of delusion. The

He added, "If they could handle things, they would be identical to the Buddha."

196

558b21–22

Master Yunmen cited:

> Whatever is as it truly is[1] contains everything.

The Master said, "So what do you call mountains, rivers, earth?"

He added, "Just these entities are all characterized by emptiness. They neither arise nor disappear and are neither defiled nor pure."[2]

197

558b23–24

The Master once held up his staff and said to the assembly:

"This staff has turned into a dragon and swallowed the whole universe. The mountains, the rivers, the earth—where are they to be found?"

Treatise on the Ceasing of Notions (Jueguanlun; Pelliot manuscript no. 2732, folio 1a) features the following dialogue:

> Question: "Do sentient beings really have mind?"
>
> Answer: "If they do have mind, they are upside-down. Deluded thoughts arise only because they posit a mind within no-mind."

[1] Ch. *zhenru,* Jap. *shinnyō:* "just so"—i.e., just as something is in itself. This expression stands for the reality of the awakened one, which is just as it is. See also section 161.

[2] The *Record of Linji* (T47: 498b29–c2) gives the following description of this state of affairs:

> Then, having entered the Dharma realm of the unborn and traveled through every country, you enter the Lotus-womb realm and realize that all entities are characterized by emptiness and that there are no real entities whatsoever.

198

At a donated meal, the Master held up his spoon and chopsticks and said: "I don't offer any food to monks from the South. I offer it only to those from the North."[1]

At the time there was a monk who asked, "Why don't you offer food to monks from the South?"

The Master replied, "Because I want to make fools of them!"

The monk inquired, "And why do you offer food to monks from the North?"

The Master answered, "One arrow, two targets."[2]

Another monk took this up and asked, "Well then, what is your opinion about [what you said] before [concerning offering food to monks from the North but not to those of the South]?"

The Master said, "All right, join the club!"

199

One time, Master Yunmen struck with his staff on a pillar and said, "Has the entirety of written Buddhist teaching managed to say it?"

The Master answered himself, "No."

[When nobody reacted] he added: "Bah! You wild fox ghosts!"

A monk inquired, "Well, how about your intention [of saying it], Master?"

The Master said, "Mr. Zhang drinks wine, and Mr. Li gets drunk."[3]

---

[1] See section 178, where Yunmen says the opposite.

[2] This corresponds to the English idiom "killing two birds with one stone."

[3] This expression is used when one person does the work while another reaps

200

558c14–16

Master Yunmen cited a national teacher who had said: "Talking about 'gradual': going against the ordinary accords with the Dao. Talking about 'immediate': there's not even the hint of a trace."[1]

Master Yunmen said, "The actions of picking up the mallet, raising the whisk, or snapping the fingers—come on, scrutinize them all![2] They too are not yet without any trace."

201

558c17–20

Once the Master held up his staff and said: "The whole universe, the earth, killing and giving life: all is in [this staff] here."

A monk then asked, "What about killing?"

The Master replied, "A total mess!"

The monk went on, "And how about giving life?"

The Master said, "[If] you want to be a rice steward . . ."[3]

---

the benefit. Yunmen criticizes the monk: "You have to say it yourself, not just get drunk on my words."

[1] Cf. *Blue Cliff Record,* case 38, T48: 175c5–6:

> When we speak about the "gradual," even to go against the ordinary is in accord with the Dao; in the bustling marketplace there is complete freedom. When we discuss the "immediate," there isn't even the hint of a trace; even a thousand sages couldn't manage to find any.

[2] These are various teaching methods of Chan masters. During the Tang dynasty, there were some famous masters who used such gestures in preference to words; the most famous may be the ninth-century Master Juzhi (Jap. Gutei), who is known for having answered all questions simply by raising his finger.

[3] The monk in charge of the preparation and cooking of the rice in a monastery. The answer seems to be part of a saying whose second phrase is left out. In this context maybe: "If you want to be a rice steward, you must cook rice. (And if you want to give life, you must not just talk about it!)"

The monk continued, "What about when one neither kills nor gives life?"

The Master got up and exclaimed, "Oh Great Perfection of Wisdom!"

558c21–22

202

The Master once said, "Meeting someone means nothing other than applying [awakening] while on the way."

Then he held up his staff and said, "The staff is not the way.[1] Neither is talk."

558c23–25

203

Master Yunmen cited [the words]: "The Dharma body eats rice,[2] and the empty phantom body is nothing other than the Dharma body."[3]

The Master said, "The whole universe and the earth: where are they? The various things cannot be gotten hold of— yet you gobble these empty [things] into your emptiness. How about investigating this? Gee, I used to think there must be something to this kind of talk!"[4]

---

[1] The character used in the original here is not that for the Way (Dao) but rather that used in "on the way."

[2] See also sections 139, 192, and 207.

[3] This is a quotation from *Yongjia's Song on Realizing the Way* (T48: 395c8). The whole line of that text reads: "[He knows that] ignorance in its true nature is nothing other than buddha-nature, [and that] this empty phantom body is nothing other than the Dharma body."

[4] Another passage of this text, which begins with the same quotation, ends with the very same words: "[Master Yunmen] quoted [the words] 'The Dharma body eats rice' [and added]: "[To say] this is already operating on [healthy] flesh and making a wound. Yet I used to think that there is something to this kind of talk!"

204

Once, the Master said: "In our tradition there is total freedom; one kills or gives life as the occasion requires."[1]

A monk asked: "How about 'killing'?"

The Master said: "Winter has gone and spring come."[2]

The monk said: "What is it like when winter has gone and spring come?"

The Master said: "Then you're making a lot of noise and ramble in all four directions of the compass with a staff across your shoulders!"

205

Addressing the assembly, Master Yunmen said:

"I let you say it any way you like, but you're not yet a descendant of our tradition. Even if you were one, it would just be noise made by a hot bowl.[3] The teachings in the twelve divisions of all three Buddhist vehicles are sleep talk, and so is Bodhidharma's coming from the West. Now if some old venerables found monasteries to explain the Buddhist teaching for the benefit of the people, there would be nothing wrong in taking a sharp sword and killing a hundred, a thousand, ten thousand of them!"

---

[1] See also section 201, and Yuanwu's introductory "pointer" to case 9 of the *Blue Cliff Record* (T48: 149a14), where the Chan master is described as follows:
> With a sharp sword in his hand, he can kill or give life as the occasion requires. . . . In the midst of death he finds life, and in the midst of life he finds death.

[2] This is likely to be a metaphor for awakening.

[3] Something without any significance. Hot bowls that are covered by a lid or that stand on a smooth surface can, because of pressure differences, make whining noises that sound surprisingly human.

He added, "Gee, I used to think there must be something to this kind of talk!"

559a8–14

206

One day the Master said: "Picking up the mallet and raising the whisk, snapping one's fingers and raising one's eyebrows, questioning and answering—all this does not match the teaching tradition of 'going beyond.' "[1]

A monk asked, "How about the teaching tradition of 'going beyond?' "

The Master replied, "[Even] the families of Jambu[2] could all answer this. But when you're for example sitting in an animated town district: do the pieces of pork that are displayed on the tables in the morning, and the vermin in the privy, hold conversations about transcending the Buddha and going beyond the founders?"

The monk said, "I wouldn't say that they do."

The Master exclaimed, "You wouldn't say that they do! If they do hold such discussions, simply saying 'they do' will not do; and if they don't hold discussions, saying 'they don't' will not do either. Such words and even what you have yourself experienced, I say this straight out, have not made it: your view is biased."

---

[1] It is interesting that the Chan tradition is so characterized here. See also the end of section 210 on p. 190.

[2] The Jambu tree (*Eugenia jambolana*) gave its name to one of the seven (or, in the Buddhist tradition, four) islands or continents surrounding the central Mt. Sumeru. Jambu can stand either for the tree or, as here, for the continent, which has the triangular shape of the Jambu tree's leaves.

207

559a15–17

Once the Master said,

"I used to say that all sounds are the Buddha's voice, all shapes are the Buddha's form,[1] and that the whole world is the Dharma body. Thus I quite pointlessly produced views that fit into the category of 'Buddhist teaching.' Right now, when I see a staff, I just call it 'staff,' and when I see a house, I just call it 'house.' "[2]

208

559a18–19

Master Yunmen once said, "It creates without creating, and it uses without using."

Then he held up his staff and said, "This isn't using without using. What is it that you call a 'staff'?"[3]

209

559a22–23

The Master brought up the saying:

All worthies without exception go by the law of wuwei[4]
—yet they do have differentiation.

---

[1] See, for example, sections 164 and 171.

[2] See section 167.

[3] Yunmen poses various questions of this sort (see, for example, sections 135, 152, 163, and 196); in general, he confronts the audience with an (often paradoxical) expression of non-duality and then goes on to probe its understanding by posing a seemingly simple question about some object.

[4] This saying, whose source is uncertain, intimates that the law of wuwei (literally "non-action") involves no differentiation. The worthies, however, are not bound by such lack of differentiation: they go by the law of wuwei and nevertheless differentiate. The import of the whole quotation seems similar to chapter 3 of the Book of Dao and De (Daodejing): "[The perfect man] acts without acting; thus everything is taken care of."

The Master added, "This staff is not the teaching of *wuwei;* nothing whatsoever is the teaching of *wuwei.*"

559a29–b4

210

Addressing the assembly, Master Yunmen said:

"Though you may have attained freedom from being obstructed by anything you encounter[1] and managed to reach the emptiness of words, phrases, and all entities—the realization that mountains, rivers, and the earth are but concepts, and that concepts cannot be grasped either—and [even if] you are equipped with so-called samadhi[2] and the 'sea of [original] nature':[3] it still is nothing but waves churning round and round without any wind. Even if you forget [dualistic] knowledge in awakening—awakening is nothing other than buddha-nature—and are called 'a man without concern,'[4] you still must realize that everything hinges on a single thing: going beyond!"[5]

559b5–8

211

Once the Master said:

"There is nothing whatsoever that does not explain the Buddhist teaching. Striking the bell or beating the drum is no

---

[1] This is quoted from a poem attributed to Master Shitou that is entitled *Merging of Difference and Identity* (Cantongqi, Jap. Sandōkai; T51: 459b19). Both in Shitou's verse and in Yunmen's address, the freedom from attachment to any object that stands opposite a watching subject is pointed out.

[2] See note to section 182.

[3] The deep and boundless sea is a metaphor for truth or true reality.

[4] The *Record of Linji* contains a passage (T47: 499b11) that contrasts the buddhas and patriarchs who are "men without concern" with people who create karma by striving and practicing.

[5] See section 206, where the Chan tradition is called "the teaching tradition of 'going beyond.' "

exception.[1] If this is the case, nothing will *be* [Buddhist teaching], and nothing will *not be*."

He added: "One should not assert that when one speaks, it *is* [the Buddhist teaching], and that when one doesn't speak, it *isn't*. Even what I just said has not quite made it. Well, as long as it benefits people, it may be okay. . . ."

212

560a15–17

One day the Master put on his long robe and said, "I'm shaking off the Dharma body."

Nobody answered.

The Master said, "Ask me!"

So a monk asked, "What does shaking off the Dharma body mean?"

The Master replied, "I see, you're getting to the point!"

213

560a17–26

Master Yunmen cited the following story by Xuansha:

> The old venerables everywhere keep talking about making use of anything to guide sentient beings. If all of a sudden they encountered someone with the three illnesses:[2] how would they deal with him? Since he is blind, he won't see

---

[1] See also case 7 of the *Blue Cliff Record* (T48: 147a22): "Whatever you pick up: there's nothing that's not it."

[2] Blindness, deafness, muteness. The Cleary brothers, as well as the majority of Japanese translators of case 88 of the *Blue Cliff Record,* think that this case is about three persons, each of whom has one of the illnesses. However, such persons would not be difficult to teach; it would be easy enough to speak to the blind, make gestures to the deaf, etc. Though that reading is also possible from the point of view of grammar, I prefer to translate this whole story on the line of one person with three illnesses.

their picking up the gavel and raising the whisk. Since he is deaf, he won't hear their most eloquent words. And since he is mute, they may want him to speak, but he cannot. So how would they deal with him? If they cannot guide him, then the Buddhist teaching has no spiritual use.

A monk asked Yunmen for instruction. The Master said: "Bow, will you!" The monk bowed and rose. Yunmen poked at him with his staff, and the monk drew back. Yunmen remarked: "Well, you're not blind." Then he told the monk to come closer again. When the monk stepped in front of him, he said: "And you're not deaf." Then Yunmen held up his staff and asked, "Do you understand?" The monk said, "I don't." And Yunmen remarked, "Neither are you mute." At this the monk attained insight.

560a27–29

214

Master Yunmen mentioned the following ancient saying:

The moment a word is brought up, the world is completely contained in it.[1]

The Master said, "Well, tell me, what word is it?"
He answered himself, "When the birds sing in springtime, they do so on the western mountain range."
Then the Master told a monk to ask him.
The monk asked, "What is that word?"
The Master said, "Hic!"[2]

---

[1] See also *Blue Cliff Record,* cases 19, 60, and 89.

[2] The Chinese character used in the original can stand for an exclamation of pain or sorrow (Oh! Alas!), but it is also used as a verb meaning "to burp," "to belch." Professor Iriya points out that this character was pronounced with a glottal stop. The translation follows this lead in conjunction with the character's verbal use.

215

560b1–3

Master Yunmen quoted a saying by Mazu:

> All words belong to the school of Kanadeva;[1] it considers
> just these to be the principal.

Master Yunmen said, "An excellent saying! Only, nobody questions me about it."

A monk then asked, "What about the school of Kanadeva?"

Master Yunmen replied, "You belong to the lowest of all ninety-six kinds [of heretics] in India!"

216

560b4–7

Master Yunmen quoted Dharma teacher [Seng] Zhao's words:

> All individual entities (dharmas) are without difference—
> [yet] one must not stretch the duck's [legs] and shorten the
> crane's,[2] level the peaks and fill up the valleys, and then
> think that they are not different![3]

---

[1] This is the fifteenth Indian patriarch, Kanadeva, who is said to have been a successor of the Indian Buddhist sage Nagarjuna. Kanadeva was by some regarded as the author of the *Hundred Treatise* (Bailun; T30, no. 1569), one of three core texts of the Chinese Madhyamika ("Three Treatise," Ch. Sanlun) tradition.

[2] See *Zhuangzi,* chapter 8:
> Though the duck's legs are short, to stretch them would make it suffer; though the crane's legs are long, to cut them shorter would make it sad. Thus: what is long by nature needs no cutting off, and what is short by nature needs no stretching.

[3] The quotation stems with insignificant differences from Seng Zhao's *Treatise on Wisdom Without Knowledge* (Banrewuzhi lun), which forms part of the famous *Treatise of Zhao* (Zhaolun, Jap. Jōron; T45, no. 1858).

193

Master Yunmen said, "The long is by nature long, the short by nature short."

Again, the Master said: "A thing occupies its position, and its mundane aspect always remains."[1]

Then he held up his staff and said, "This staff is not a thing that always remains, is it?"[2]

560b8–10

217

Master Yunmen mentioned an old saying: "Even a single thought contains perfect wisdom."

The Master held up his staff and said, "The whole universe is on top of this staff. If you can penetrate it, there isn't any staff in sight either. Even so, you'd still be in bad shape."[3]

560b16–19

218

Master Yunmen related [the legend according to which] the Buddha, immediately after his birth, pointed with one hand to heaven and with the other to earth, walked a circle in seven steps, looked at the four quarters, and said, "Above heaven and under heaven, I alone am the Honored One."

The Master said, "Had I witnessed this at the time, I would have knocked him dead with one stroke and fed him to the dogs in order to bring about peace on earth!"

---

[1] This is a phrase often quoted by Chan masters; in slightly different form, it is also found in the second chapter of the *Lotus Sutra*.

[2] A play on words may also be involved here: the characters that are translated as "always remains" are also a technical term meaning "monastery property."

[3] See the story about Zhaozhou on p. 64.

219

561a3–5

Master Yunmen related the following story:

> Changqing[1] asked the Genius,[2] "The Buddhist teachings
> say that sentient beings use it every day yet do not know it.
> The Confucian texts also state that one uses it daily yet
> does not know it. Now what is that which one does not
> know?" The Genius replied, "One does not know the
> Great Way."

Master Yunmen said, "Exactly, he doesn't know!"

220

561a8–9

Master Yunmen mentioned that Changqing[3] had seized his staff
and said, "If you're able to know this [staff], your life's study is
accomplished."

The Master said, "You're able to—so why don't you leave
it at that?"

221

561a10–13

Master Yunmen mentioned the following anecdote:

> When Yunyan[4] was sweeping the floor, Daowu[5] said to
> him: "What good is so much petty effort?"

---

[1] Changqing Huileng (854–932), a co-disciple of Yunmen under Master
Xuefeng Yicun.

[2] Chang Zhuo the Genius. See section 188, note 1.

[3] Changqing Huileng. See note to previous section.

[4] Yunyan Tansheng (Jap. Ungan Donjō; 780?–841).

[5] Daowu Yuanzhi (769–835).

Yunyan replied, "You ought to know that there is one who doesn't [make such a useless effort]!"

Daowu said: "Well, that's already a second moon!"

Yunyan held up the broom and said, "Which moon is this?"

Daowu shook his sleeves and went out.

Master Yunmen remarked, "When a slave meets his peer, they commiserate each other."

Statements With Answers in Place of the Audience

■ ■ ■

222

Master Yunmen asked a monk, "Are Korea and China the same or different?"

Master Yunmen answered on behalf of the monk, "The Monks' Hall, the Buddha Hall, the kitchen pantry, the main gate."[1]

223

In the hall, Master Yunmen said,

"Tell me, what level of activity is it when the old buddhas do it[2] with the pillars?"

---

[1] See also section 245, where the kitchen pantry and main gate appear in another context, and section 272, which addresses the problem of identity and difference. The latter must be seen in the context of not-twoness as explained in section 275: "All objects are no-objects; just this is called 'all objects.' " This thought has been formulated in various other ways. The modern Japanese philosopher Kitarō Nishida, for example, coined the term "absolutely contradictory self-identity," D. T. Suzuki spoke of the "logic of as-it-is-it-is-not" (*sokuhi no ronri*), and R. DeMartino uses the term "nondualistic-duality" (see p. 64).

[2] Literally, to cross, to have relations with. This term has a strong sexual conno-

Nobody answered.

The Master said, "Ask me, I'll tell you!"

A monk asked [what level of function it was], and the Master answered, "One silk sash: thirty in cash."[1]

In place of the first words [about buddhas and pillars], the Master said, "When clouds gather on South Mountain, rain falls on North Mountain."[2]

The monk went on inquiring, "How about 'one silk sash: thirty in cash'?"

The Master replied, "It's a deal!"[3]

561c21–22

224

One day Master Yunmen said, "What is it that you deliberate about and concentrate upon?"

In place of the monks, Master Yunmen answered, "Salt is expensive, rice is cheap."

561c22–23

225

Once Master Yunmen said, "What is accomplished when one has mentioned the two words 'Buddha' and 'Dharma'?"

He answered in place of the audience, "Dead frogs!"[4]

---

tation, which may very well be present here in order to attack the masters who constantly used such pillars in their teaching.

[1] It is not clear whether this was a considerable amount of money or not. Some sexual implication may again be present (for example, the amount of money needed for the services of a prostitute?).

[2] In Chinese tradition, the image of clouds and rain is commonly used for the sexual act.

[3] This expression was used at auctions to make a buyer's decision final.

[4] In the Chan tradition, frogs can stand for people who make a lot of noise yet have little to say.

226

One day Master Yunmen said, "The ancient ones faced the wall and shut the gate.[1] But could they break through [this] in here?"[2]

In place of his audience, Yunmen said, "What a dry piece of shit is [this] in here!"

He added, "One."[3]

227

Master Yunmen entered the Dharma Hall, and when the assembly had gathered and settled down, he said, "There's a big mistake;[4] check it out most thoroughly."

He said in place of the monks, "[For this] there's no need for someone else."[5]

---

[1] This is a reference to Bodhidharma, who reputedly sat facing a wall for years after coming to China, and to the Buddha, who reputedly shut himself in at Magadha and did not want to speak because of the ultimate ineffability of the Dharma.

[2] One could imagine that Yunmen pointed to his chest while he spoke these words.

[3] As with other one-word answers, the possibilities for translating are manifold. One could also translate this by "the One" or "unity," etc.

[4] Master Dahui once said (*Record of Dahui,* T47: 894b6 ff.):

> What does "mistake" mean? It is to be taken in by form, sound, scent, taste, touch, and separate entities, and not being able to detach oneself from them. It is seeking knowledge and looking for understanding in the words and phrases of the scriptural teachings and of ancient worthies.

[5] See also Yunmen's earlier statement that this matter is one's very own matter where no one else can take one's place (end of section 46).

562a13–14

228

The Master once asked a monk, "How are you doing?"
In place of the monk he replied, "I'm hungry!"

562a18–22

229

Instructing the assembly, Master Yunmen said, "It is mentioned once and is not talked about anymore. How about that which is mentioned once?"

He continued, "If you're not in accord with it, seek some way in! Even having buddhas numberless as specks of dust on your tongue and the holy teachings of the entire Buddhist canon under your feet is nowhere near as good as awakening! Now is there anyone who is awakened? Come forward and try expressing it!"

In place of the silent assembly he said, "That's what you're faced with when you have children."

With regard to the first words (about bringing it up once) he said in place of his listeners, "Though the capital Changan is pleasant, [it is not a place for a long stay]."[1]

562a27–b1

230

While picking tea, the Master said, "Picking tea is tiresome. Come on, ask me a question!"

When nobody responded, he continued, "If you can't say

---

[1] The full form of this saying appears in case 64 of the *Blue Cliff Record* (T48: 195b14).

anything, recite the ABC.[1] And if you're not up to that, trace characters!"[2]

In place of the silent audience, he said, "Might be worth a try. . . ."

Responding to the first words ["picking tea is tiresome"], he said in place of his audience, "I toil, yet it doesn't come to anything."

231

In the hall, the Master raised his staff and said, "Hey, look! The entire cosmos is shaking, all at once!"[3] Then he descended from his seat.

In place of the silent audience he said, "Heave-ho!"

232

Once Master Yunmen said, "What is a statement that does not fool people?"[4]

In place of his listeners he said, "Don't tell me that this was one that did!"

---

[1] In the original, these are not the first letters of the alphabet, of course, but the first three of a row of simple characters that, according to legend, young Confucius wrote to his father. From the mid-Tang era, they were used for teaching the art of writing to beginners.

[2] When learning to write, Chinese children used to trace the instructor's red characters and overwrite them in black ink.

[3] In Buddhist texts, the universe is often said to have trembled when an eminent person stated a profound truth.

[4] A Chinese proverb says: "Good talk does not fool people; if it does, it's not good talk."

233

One day the Master said, "When you exert your whole strength, what do you say?"

In place of the monks, Yunmen said, "Five sesame buns and three bowls of tea!"

234

Once the Master asked, "What is the question that lays it all out?"

In place of the asked monk, Yunmen answered, "Whack the monk next to me!"

235

Once, when the Master had finished talking, he stood up, banged his staff down on his meditation chair, and said, "With so many word-creepers[1] up to now, what place will I be banished to? Clever chaps understand, but stupid ones are being completely fooled by me."[2]

Instead of the listeners, the Master said, "Putting frost on top of snow."

236

Once the Master said, "The Buddhist teaching does not need to be fixed in words; [but tell me:] what is most valuable in the world?"

---

[1] See section 46, p. 108, note 2.

[2] The word "me" (wo) of the Taipei edition is correct; the Taishō text has a misprint here.

In place of his listeners, Yunmen said: "Don't tell me this is dime-a-dozen!"

He added, "A dry piece of shit!"

237

Addressing the assembly, Master Yunmen said, "Look, look! I got killed!"

Pretending to collapse, he said, "Do you understand?"

238

One day the Master said, "I entangle myself in words with you every day; I can't go on till the night. Come on, ask me a question right here and now!"

In place of his listeners, Master Yunmen said, "I'm just afraid that Reverend Yunmen won't answer."

239

Once the Master said, "What is the one phrase under your very feet?"

Instead of his audience he said, "Is there one?"

240

One day the Master said, "I'm not asking you about putting aside [the ultimate truth of] the Buddha Dharma. But is there someone here who knows about conventional truth?"[1]

---

[1] The doctrine of the "two truths" plays such a prominent role in Buddhism that already the Indian sage Nagarjuna remarked (*Madhyamaka Kārikā* 24:8,9; translation from Mervyn Sprung, ed., *The Problem of Two Truths in Buddhism and Vedānta* [Dordrecht, Netherlands: Reidel, 1973], p. 57):

In place of his audience he said, "If I say there is such a thing I'll be arrested by the Reverend Yunmen."

563b4–5

241

Once Master Yunmen said, "When Bodhidharma came from the West, why did he have trouble getting successors?"

In place of the silent audience he said, "Oh, come off it!"

563b5–8

242

When the Master had once finished talking, he stood up and said, "If tonight you understand it all, get up early, seize a sword, and lop off my head: that will be the end of my chatter!" Then he pulled up[1] his robe, shook it, and said, "How about this?"[2]

In place of a monk he said, "I must not let you down, Master."[3]

The buddhas teach *dharma* (the doctrine) by resorting to two truths: One is the conventional or provisional truth, the other is the ultimate truth.

Those who do not comprehend the distinction between these two truths do not comprehend the deep significance in the Buddha's teachings.

The conventional truth corresponds to that which to the dualistic mind seems true, while ultimate or genuine truth refers to that which is evident to the awakened mind.

[1] One pulls up the robe when taking it off.

[2] Professor Iriya suggests that Yunmen acts as if he were already dead, picks up and shakes a dead monk's robe, and thus mocks the audience for being unable to finish him off.

[3] A similar point is made in section 247.

243

Addressing the assembly, Master Yunmen said, "I'm not asking you about before the fifteenth day; try to say something about after the fifteenth day!"[1]

Yunmen himself answered on behalf of the listeners, "Every day is a good day!"[2]

244

In the Dharma Hall, the Master was silent for a long time and then said, "I'm making a terrible fool of myself." With that he left his seat.

In place of the monks he said, "Aha, not just us!"

245

Once the Master cited a man of old[3] who had said,

---

[1] It is not clear what Yunmen means by the "fifteenth day" (middle of the lunar month). Since the fifteenth is one of the two monthly fast days with confession and repentance ceremonies (during which the faults and transgressions of the previous half-month were confessed and repented before the whole monastic community), Yunmen could mean: "I don't want to hear about [your transgressions] of the last half-month; tell me about [your resolutions for] the coming half-month." Charles Luk wrote that the fifteenth day is the full-moon day; the full moon symbolizes enlightenment (*Zen and Ch'an Teachings, Second Series*, p. 198).

[2] See also section 257.

[3] The man quoted here is Tanxia Tianren (739–824), and the quotation is part of a long verse contained in the *Collection from the Founder's Halls* (1.161,6). See also section 143.

Each and every person has the radiant light—[yet] when it is looked at, it is not seen: dark and obscure. What about that radiant light?[1]

On behalf of the silent audience he said, "The kitchen pantry, the main gate."[2]

He added, "I'd rather have nothing!"[3]

563b25–27

246

At a donated meal the Master asked a monk, "Forget about all the phrases that you've ever learned in the monasteries and tell me: how does my food taste?"

On behalf of the silent monks he said, "There's too little salt and vinegar on the vegetables."

563c13–15

247

Once he said, "Just you, all of you, are on pilgrimage and must know that there is a way in. Now is there anyone who is able to express it in words? Come forward and try saying it!"

---

[1] Master Yuanwu cites in his comments to Yunmen's words the following verse from Shitou's *Merging of Difference and Identity* (T51: 459c15–16):

Just within this light there is darkness
But don't confront it as darkness.
And within darkness there is light
But don't meet it as light.

[2] See section 222 and its note.

[3] There is an interesting story about Master Zhaozhou where this expression is used in a similar way: When Master Zhaozhou saw a monk perform the customary bow, he gave him a blow with his staff. The monk said: "To bow is a good thing, isn't it?" Master Zhaozhou replied, "I'd rather have nothing!" (*Record of Zhaozhou*, ZZ119: 166d1).

On behalf of the silent audience he said, "I, too, shouldn't let the Master down."[1]

248

The Master said to the assembly:

> Within, there is a jewel. It is hidden inside the human body.[2]

He said: "I pick up the lantern inside the Buddha Hall and place the main monastery gate on top of it. How about that?"

As no one answered he replied on behalf of the audience, "If one chases after things, one's intentions are swept along."

He added, "The thunder rolls, and clouds are gathering."[3]

249

Master Yunmen addressed the assembly, saying, "I don't want any words from our tradition. [Now tell me in your own words:] What is 'self' in the teaching of our patriarchal school?"

In their place he simply extended both hands.

250

When a monk came for instruction, the Master lifted his robe and said, "If you can put it in words, you fall into the trap of my

---

[1] Yunmen possibly advances an answer that skillfully avoids the question, and he thereby probably castigates his listeners for being concerned only about their relationship with the teacher.

[2] This is a saying of Seng Zhao.

[3] These are signs of a looming disaster.

robe. If you cannot, then you're sitting in a demon's cave. What do you do?"

He answered on behalf of the monk, "I'm exhausted."

564c17–18

251

Once Master Yunmen asked, "What's wrong with someone who is in the dark about himself?"

He answered on behalf of the silent monks, "That ought not to be a problem for a great man!"

564c20–22

252

One day Master Yunmen said, "If you're sitting [in the meditation hall] underneath your robe and bowl,[1] I'm tying you up deadly. And if you come running up [to the Dharma Hall], I have you run to death. What is a phrase that'll get you out of this fix?"

He said on behalf of the listeners, "Quick!"

565a17–19

253

Once the Master said, "In the lands of all ten directions there is nothing but the teaching of the unique vehicle. Tell me, is your self inside or outside the teaching of the unique vehicle?"

On behalf of the silent audience he said, "Come in!"

He added, "There you are!"

---

[1] The monk's robe and bowl were stored over his meditation seat. Robe and bowl also stand for all worldly possessions of a monk.

254

One day he said, "You take being as being.[1] How can you avoid that?"

On behalf of the monks he said, "Tough luck!"

255

Once Master Yunmen said, "It's so difficult to find out where the problem lies!"

On behalf of the monks he said, "Find out!"

256

The Master once said, "Do you see?"

He answered himself, "I see."

He went on, "What do you see?"

On behalf of those present he replied, "A flower."

257

One day he said, "It's eleven days since you entered the summer meditation period. Well, have you gained an entry? What do you say?"

On behalf of the monks he replied, "Tomorrow is the twelfth."[2]

---

[1] This stands in contrast to the awakened view as expressed in the quotation from the *Diamond Sutra* in section 275. See also the note to section 222.

[2] This answer could point towards a possible but unorthodox interpretation of section 243, which can also be read as a reproach for continued procrastination.

258

Once Master Yunmen mentioned an ancient's saying:

What enters by the gate is not your home treasure.[1]

Then Yunmen asked, "What about the gate?"
He answered on behalf of the monks, "Even if I were able to say it, it would be of no use."

259

The Master once said, "I'm not asking you for verbal teachings of our tradition. This is heaven. That is earth." Pointing to himself he said, "This is me." Pointing to the pillar he said, "That's a pillar. What is Buddhist teaching?"
On behalf of the silent audience he said, "That's very difficult, too. . . ."

260

One day Master Yunmen said,
"People learning the Buddhist teaching are numerous like sand grains on the River Ganges. Come on, make a statement from the tips of the hundred weeds!"[2]
On behalf of the silent assembly he said, "All!"

---

[1] See *Record of Linji,* T47: 497b16–17 (Sasaki translation, p. 8):
If you wish to differ in no way from the Patriarch-Buddha, just don't seek outside.

[2] The hundred weeds stand for the infinite variety of phenomena in which the teaching of the Buddha manifests itself fully. An awakened person ought to be able "to point out the wondrous mind of nirvana on the tips of the hundred weeds" (Master Yuanwu's pointer to case 59 of the *Blue Cliff Record,* T48: 191c14–15).

261

566a21–22

Once Master Yunmen said, "I want to be told neither about before today nor about after today: come on, tell me something just about today!"

On behalf of the audience he said, "Now's the time!"

262

566b18–19

One day Master Yunmen said, "Come on, pose me a question outside the Buddhist teaching!"

On behalf of the monks he replied, "Even one is too much."

263

567a4–6

When Master Yunmen saw a monk come to visit him, he struck a blow on a pillar and said, "You came in here to deceive me!"

On behalf of the monk he answered, "[Lucky me,] he only hit the pillar."

Master Yunmen whacked the monk and said, "Letting off steam for other people's benefit."

Critical Examinations

■ ■ ■

567c5–7

264

The Master asked a monk, "Where have you been?"

The monk replied, "I've been harvesting tea."

The Master asked, "Do people pick the tea, or does the tea pick people?"

The monk had no answer.

In his place, Master Yunmen answered, "The Master has said it all; there's nothing I can add."

567c7–10

265

Master Yunmen asked a monk, "Are you the monastery's repairman?"

The monk said yes.

The Master said, "The whole universe is a house. How about the master of the house?"

The monk had no answer.

The Master said, "Ask me, I'll tell you."

The monk asked, and the Master replied, "He has passed away."

On behalf of the monk he replied to the first question, "How many people has he deceived?"

266

The Master asked a monk, "Where do you come from?"

The monk replied, "I have paid my respects to [the Sixth Patriarch's] stupa."

The Master inquired, "What did he tell you?"

The monk asked back, "What do you say, Master?"

Master Yunmen said, "And I was under the impression that you're a clever lad!"

The monk had no answer.

Master Yunmen replied on the monk's behalf, "I only did what's right and proper!"[1]

267

The Master asked a monk, "Do you see the lantern?"[2]

The monk replied, "I can't see it anymore."

The Master said, "The monkey is attached to a pillar."[3]

Yunmen replied in place of the monk, "I'm deeply grateful to receive the profound heart of your Buddhist teaching, Master."

To the first question he replied on behalf of the monk, "I'd rather have nothing!"

---

[1] This refers to the Confucian cardinal virtues of *ren* and *yi,* humaneness and righteousness.

[2] The Taishō text has here "Is there a lantern?"; my translation follows the Taipei edition.

[3] The monk wants to assert that the lantern is no longer an object that stands opposite him—i.e., that he has become one with it. The monkey often stands for the human mind, which restlessly moves from object to object. The master thus lets the monk know what he thinks of his kind of oneness or samadhi: it is no more than the freedom of an attached monkey.

268

At a meal Master Yunmen asked a monk, "The broth gets absorbed by the rice and the rice by the broth. Where lies the problem? If you can tell, we'll discuss it further."

The monk had no answer.

The Master replied in place of the monk, "Good broth, good rice."

He added, "Don't say that [this is talk by a] reverend in a frog's hole."[1]

269

When Master Yunmen saw the characters that mean "dragon treasury," he asked a monk, "What is it that can come out of the dragon's treasury?"[2]

The monk had no answer.

The Master said, "Ask me, I'll tell you!"

So the monk asked, and the Master replied, "What comes out is a dead frog."

On behalf of the [baffled] monk he said, "A fart!"

Again, he said, "Steam-breads and steam-cookies."

270

Master Yunmen asked a monk, "Where do you come from?"

The monk replied, "From the Chen district [in Hunan]."

The Master asked, "And where did you spend your summer [period of monastic practice]?"

---

[1] See section 225, p. 198, note 4.

[2] This treasury stands for the Buddhist canon, which is guarded by a dragon. The question thus means something like: What can come out of the Buddhist teaching?

The monk: "At Master Xichan's."

Yunmen inquired, "What teaching does he expound?"

The monk opened his hands and let them dangle on both sides.

The Master struck him.

The monk said, "I'm [still] speaking!"

The Master opened his hands.

The monk had no response.

The Master struck him and chased him out.

In place of the monk he said, "I'm going, I am!"

271

570c2–6

The Master asked a monk who was reading a Buddhist scripture, "What's the title on the cover?"

The monk held up the scripture.

The Master said, "I've got that, too!"

The monk said, "Since you've got it, why do you ask?"

The Master replied, "How can I help [asking]?"

The monk inquired, "What's the problem?"

The Master said, "You don't notice the stench of your own shit!"

In place of the [dumbfounded] monk, Yunmen retorted, "Today I noticed that for the first time!"

He added: "Deshan's staff and Zihu's dog!"[1]

---

[1] Master Deshan was known for his saying: "If you can put it in words, you get twenty blows, and if you cannot you also get twenty blows." The story of Master Zihu is told in case 96 of the *Blue Cliff Record* (T48: 219c2–5):

> Master Zihu set up a sign on his outer gate; the sign said, "Zihu has a dog: above, he grabs people's heads; in the middle, he grabs people's loins; below, he grabs people's legs. If you hesitate, you lose your body and life!" Whenever Zihu saw a newcomer, he would immediately shout, "Watch out for the dog!" As soon as

And further: "Reverend, this question of yours is dead-clever!"

570c25–28

272

Master Yunmen asked a monk, "An old man said, 'In the realm of non-dualism there is not the slightest obstacle between self and other.' What about Japan and Korea in this context?"

The monk said, "They are not different."

The Master remarked, "You go to hell."

In place [of the monk, Yunmen] said, "One must not produce hell-views."

He added, "How can one get the jewel and return?"[1]

572a23–64

273

Master Yunmen asked a monk, "Where have you just come from?"

The monk[2] said, "From Chadu [in Jiangxi province]."

Yunmen inquired, "Where have you practiced during the summer?"

The monk replied, "In the Baoci monastery in Hunan province."

Yunmen asked, "And when did you leave there?"

The monk answered, "In August."

---

the monk turned his head, Zihu would immediately return to the abbot's room.

[1] Getting the jewel from the dragon king at the bottom of the sea and returning back home is a metaphor for reaching the essence of Buddhist teaching and applying it in daily life.

[2] Other sources make it clear that the monk in question was a disciple of Yunmen by the name of Dongshan Shouchu (910–990).

Master Yunmen remarked: "I spare you the three score blows of the staff [that you deserve]."[1]

The next day the monk came to see the Master and said to him: "Yesterday I was spared sixty blows by you, Master, but I have no idea what I was guilty of."

The Master cried: "You rice bag! Jiangxi, Hunan, and you still go on this way?!"

At these words the monk had the great awakening. Then he said, "Hereafter I'll go to a place where there are no human hearths and will build myself a grass hut. I won't grow a single grain of rice nor store a single bunch of vegetables, and I will receive the sages that will come and go from all directions. I'll pull out the nails and pegs for them, tear off their greasy hats, strip off their stinking jackets, and I'll see to it that they get clean and free and become [real] patch-robed monks. Isn't this superb?"

Yunmen shot back, "You rice bag! You're the size of a coconut yet you open such a big mouth!"

274

572b23–25

Master Yunmen asked a monk, "Are you going to gather firewood today?"

The monk said, "Yes."

The Master said, "An ancient has said, 'Even if you don't see a single object, your eyeball is there.' "

While gathering firewood, [Master Yunmen] threw down a piece of wood and said, "All Buddhist scriptures explain just this."

---

[1] Sixty blows of the staff would be an extremely harsh, possibly even deadly, punishment.

572b27–c1

275

The Master asked a monk, "Are you reading the *Diamond Sutra?*"

The monk replied, "Yes."

Quoting this scripture the Master said,

All objects (dharmas) are no-objects; just this is called "all objects."

Then he held up his fan and said, "You call this a fan. That's a concept. I hold it up—but where is it? What good is it to be overwhelmed by delusive thoughts from morning till night?"

572c3–7

276

When Master Yunmen once saw a monk reading a scripture he said, "To read scriptures, one must be equipped with the scripture-reading eye. The lantern, the pillar, and the entire Buddhist canon lack nothing."

Holding up his staff, he continued, "The entire Buddhist canon is right on the tip of this staff. Come on, where do you see a single dot? Yet [the canon] is wide open:

Thus I have heard: The lands in all ten directions, encompassing the worlds as numerous as grains of sands . . ."[1]

572c12–15

277

Master Yunmen asked a monk, "Who made this sesame bread?"

The monk held it up.

---

[1] The master read these words (that are common at the beginning of Buddhist scriptures) from the tip of his staff.

The Master said, "Put that aside; that's something you've learned on the meditation platform. Who made this sesame bread?"

The monk said, "Master, you had better not deceive me!"

The Master said, "You numskull!"

Pilgrimage Record

■ ■ ■

278

Yunmen first called on Chan master Muzhou Daozong.[1] The moment Muzhou saw Yunmen approach he shut the door. Thereupon Yunmen knocked at the door, and Muzhou asked: "Who is it?"

Yunmen replied, "It's me!"

Muzhou asked, "What are you here for?"

Yunmen said, "I am not yet clear about myself. Please, Master, give me guidance!"

Muzhou opened the door, cast one glance, shut it again, and withdrew.

In this manner Yunmen went to knock at the door on three consecutive days. On the third day, when Muzhou set out to open the door, Yunmen forced his way in. Muzhou seized him and said: "Say it, say it!"

Yunmen hesitated.

Muzhou pushed him out, saying, "Utterly useless stuff."[2]

Through this Yunmen attained awakening.

---

[1] Muzhou was Yunmen's first Chan teacher. See p. 19 ff.

[2] Literally, "Stone drills from the Qin period." See the explanation on p. 20.

279

When Yunmen arrived at the village at the foot of Mt. Xuefeng, he met a monk whom he asked: "Will the reverend go up the mountain today?"

The monk said yes, and Yunmen said, "I entrust you with a case to ask abbot Xuefeng, but you must not say that these are someone else's words!"

The monk consented, and Yunmen continued: "After your arrival at the monastery you will see the abbot take the high seat in the Dharma Hall to give a formal sermon. As soon as the assembly has gathered, go forward and say at once: 'Hey, old lad, why don't you rid yourself of the iron cangue around your neck?' "[1]

The monk followed Yunmen's instructions exactly. When Xuefeng heard the monk talk like this he descended from his seat, blocked his chest, seized him, and said: "Tell me, tell me, quick!"

When the monk did not answer Xuefeng let him loose and said, "The words you said were not yours." The monk insisted that they were. But when Xuefeng said, "Attendant, bring me a rope and a stick, will you!," the monk admitted: "They were not my words but those of a monk from Zhejiang down in the village. He instructed me to come and say what I said." Xuefeng said, "You of the assembly, go to the village and welcome this spiritual guide of five hundred persons!"

The following day Yunmen ascended the mountain. As soon as Xuefeng saw him, he asked, "What enabled you to reach such a state?" Yunmen lowered his head. After this they were like two matching pieces of a tally.[2]

---

[1] Wooden or iron cangues were used for constraining criminals.

[2] Tallies (such as a broken piece of wood whose two pieces fit into each other

280

A monk asked, "What is that which goes beyond the Dharma body?"

Master Yunmen replied, "It's all very well for you to talk about 'beyond.' But what do you mean by 'Dharma body'?"

"Please, Master, consider [what I asked]!"

Yunmen said: "Well, let's leave considerations aside for now. How does the Dharma body speak?"

"Like this, like this!"

Yunmen remarked, "That's something you could cook up on the long [meditation] bench. Let me ask you: Can the Dharma body eat rice?"

The monk was speechless.

281

Master Sushan[1] said to his assembly: "Before the Xiantong years,[2] I could understand only what is at the margin of the body of teaching (Dharma body). Since the Xiantong years, I am able to understand that which goes beyond the Dharma body."

Yunmen asked, "I heard you say that before the Xiantong years, you could understand only what is at the margin of the Dharma body and that after the Xiantong years you could understand that which goes beyond the Dharma body. Is that correct?"

---

perfectly) were used as identification badges and proof of authorization. For a less embroidered account of this meeting, see p. 22. This and some other stories of the Pilgrimage Record show unmistakable traces of later editorial activity.

[1] Sushan Guangren (837–909) was a Dharma heir of Master Dongshan Liangjie, one of the founders of the Caodong/Sōtō tradition of Zen.

[2] These are the years between 860 and 873. During this period Sushan practiced under Master Dongshan Liangjie. Thus this means: "Before I practiced under Master Dongshan . . ."

Sushan said yes.

Yunmen asked, "So what is at the margin of the Dharma body?"

Sushan replied, "Withered camellias."

Yunmen: "And what is beyond the Dharma body?"

Sushan answered, "No withered camellias."

Yunmen asked, "May I explain the reason?"

Sushan said, "Go ahead!"[1]

Yunmen said, "Withered camellias reveal what is at the margin of the Dharma body, and no withered camellias reveal what is beyond the Dharma body, don't they?"

Sushan replied: "Yes, they do."

Yunmen asked, "But the Dharma body embraces everything, doesn't it?"

Sushan answered, "How wouldn't it?"

Yunmen pointed at a water pitcher[2] and said, "Does the Dharma body embrace this?"

Sushan said, "Monk, don't just understand what is at the margin of the water pitcher!"

Yunmen bowed.

282

574a21–26

Yunmen visited Caoshan.[3] Caoshan instructed his community as follows: "People everywhere all just adopt set patterns. Why

---

[1] Such a permission is rare in Chan records and already implies high esteem of Yunmen; in general, a question of this kind would be answered with a stick.

[2] This "pure" pitcher was used for cleaning the monks' hands.

[3] Caoshan Benji (Jap. Sōzan Honjaku; 840–901) and his teacher Dongshan Liangjie (Jap. Tōzan Ryōkai; 807–869) are revered as the founders of the Caodong/Sōtō tradition of Zen.

don't you tell them a turning phrase[1] in order to make them get rid of their doubt?"

Yunmen asked Caoshan: "Why is it that one does not know of the existence of that which is most immediate?"

Caoshan: "Just because it is the most immediate!"

Yunmen: "And how can one become truly intimate with it?"

Caoshan: "By not turning towards it."

Yunmen: "But can one know the most immediate if one does not face it?"

Caoshan: "It's then that one knows it best."

Yunmen consented: "Exactly, exactly!"

574a26–b1

283

Yunmen asked Caoshan, "What is the practice of a monk?"

Caoshan replied, "Eating rice from the monastery fields."

Yunmen said, "And if one does just that?"

Caoshan replied, "Can you really eat it?"

Yunmen said, "Yes, I can."

Caoshan: "How do you do that?"

Yunmen: "What is difficult about putting on clothes and eating rice?"

Caoshan said, "Why don't you say that you're wearing a hide and have horns [like an animal]?"

Yunmen bowed.

---

[1] Such phrases have the power to throw people out of their dualistic tracks and trigger awakening.

284

When Master Yunmen went to see Tiantong,[1] Tiantong said, "Have you managed to settle it?"

Master Yunmen asked back, "What are you saying, Reverend?"

Tiantong replied, "If you *haven't* understood, then you're involved in all that is in front of you."

Master Yunmen said, "If you *have* understood, then you're involved in all that is in front of you!"

285

Yunmen said to Ganfeng,[2] "Teacher, I request an answer!"

Ganfeng asked: "Have you come to me yet?"

Yunmen replied, "So I'm late."

Ganfeng said, "Oh, is that so? Is that so?"

Yunmen shot back, "I always thought you were a crook; but now I realize you're even worse!"[3]

---

[1] This is probably one of two men among Dongshan Liangjie's disciples who carried this name.

[2] Yuezhou Ganfeng was a Dharma heir of Dongshan Liangjie (807–869).

[3] Literally: "I always thought you were Houbai, but you're Houhei!" The commentary to case 40 of the *Record of Serenity* points out that this is a proverb; Houbai (literally, "monkey-white") was a crook and liar of considerable talent, and the invented Houhei (literally, "monkey-black") is presumably even worse. Such abuse is in Chan texts often the highest form of praise.

■ ■ ■

Materials

■ ■ ■

Major Sources
For Yunmen's
Life and Teaching
■ ■ ■

A. The two inscriptions that were carved in stone in 959 and 964, ten and fifteen years, respectively, after Yunmen's death.

B. The *Record of Yunmen,* which is partially translated in this volume.

C. Some texts of the "Transmission of the Lamp" genre, especially the two following collections:

1) the *Collection from the Founder's Halls* (Ch. Zutangji, Kor. Chodang chip, Jap. Sodōshū), which was completed in 952, only three years after Yunmen's death.

2) the *Jingde Era Record of the Transmission of the Lamp* (Ch. Jingde chuandenglu, Jap. Keitoku dentōroku), which appeared in 1004.

D. The explanations about 209 difficult terms from the *Record of Yunmen,* contained in the *Collection of Items from the Garden of the Patriarchs* (Ch. Zutingshiyuan, Jap. Soteijien).

   Of course, many additional sources from later times were also consulted. They are referred to in more detail in the edition for specialists mentioned on p. xvi.

The Stone Inscriptions

The first of the two stone inscriptions that are preserved in Yunmen's monastery was written on January 12, 959—i.e., ten years after the

229

master's death. The author, Lei Yue, was a high official of the government of the Southern Han empire. While two sources bear an earlier date, one of them[1] contributes little to the biography of Yunmen, and the second[2] actually appears (in spite of its early date) to be the product of a later age. The stone inscription of 959 is thus probably the oldest extensive biographical document about Master Yunmen. It contains a long introduction in which the master is portrayed as a true successor to the Buddha and the Chan founding fathers. This is followed by the biographical part, which served as the major source of the biography given in this volume. It closes with a description of the burial ceremony.

The second stone inscription stems from the hand of another imperial official, a man by the name of Chen Shouzhong. It is dated May 15, 964, and its writing was triggered by a miracle. Chen writes that the magistrate Ruan Shaozhuang saw Yunmen in a dream and was given the order to open the grave stupa. When, after the necessary bureaucratic procedures and approval from higher authorities, the grave site was opened, Yunmen's body was found in a mummified state. It was soon brought to the capital Guangzhou (Canton), where it was displayed and worshiped for a whole month. Apart from this, the content of the second inscription is quite congruent with that of the first, which was written five years earlier.

The Lamp Histories

The two Chan compendia, the *Collection from the Founder's Halls* (952) and the *Jingde Era Record of the Transmission of the Lamp* (1004), are close enough in time to Yunmen to be of considerable value, both with

---

[1] The *Collection from the Founder's Halls* (Ch. Zutangji), which appeared in 952.

[2] This is the biography of the master (T47: 575c3–576a18) that is dated from May 25, 949, the day of Master Yunmen's burial ceremony. Its author is Lei Yue, the man who ten years later also wrote the first stone inscription. The parallels between the two documents are strong, but the supposedly earlier biography includes ostensibly later legends and was probably rewritten (or even written) at a much later point in time.

respect to what they contain about the life and teaching of Yunmen and what they do not.

The *Collection from the Founder's Halls* is of special interest, since it originated in circles around Yunmen's teacher Xuefeng and was probably not rewritten by later editors until it was rediscovered in Korea in the early twentieth century. In light of the fact that Yunmen died only three years before this text was completed, the amount of information about him is surprisingly large and of great research value.

The *Jingde Era Record of the Transmission of the Lamp* became a model for later Chan texts of this genre; it contains substantial information about the life and teaching of Yunmen. This text (and, of course, the *Record of Yunmen* as well) went through the hands of successive editors and was in the process altered to various degrees. Only detailed research of the history of a text can reveal what form and extent such changes had.

The History of the
Record of Yunmen[1]

■ ■ ■

The Edition Used for This Translation

The *Record of Yunmen* is the main source for the teaching of Master Yunmen. This text has come down to us in various editions, the oldest of which is stored in the Taiwanese National Central Library in Taipei. It forms part of a larger collection of Chan records entitled *Record of the Sayings of Old Worthies* (Ch. Guzunsu yulu, Jap. Kosonshuku goroku), which dates from the year 1267. This unpunctuated and most reliable edition of the *Record of Yunmen* was used for the translation. It is hard to obtain; therefore, for the convenience of scholars and readers of Chinese, I keyed all references to the most widely available edition of the *Record of Yunmen,* the one that is found in the Taishō edition of the Chinese canon (Taishō shinshū daizōkyō; volume 47, text number 1988). Though the Taishō edition features many mistakes of punctuation and a number of variant forms of Chinese characters, the Chinese text itself is, with the exception of some different colophons and a few typesetting mistakes, almost identical with the older edition stored in Taipei. Important differences between the two editions are pointed out in the notes to the translation.

The oldest extant edition of the *Record of Yunmen* was thus

---

[1] For a more detailed history of this text, see my article "The Making of a Chan Record" in *Annual Report from the Institute for Zen Studies* (Zenbunka kenkyūjo kiyō) 17 (1991), pp. 1–90.

printed more than three hundred years after Master Yunmen's death. However, we are lucky to have some older source materials that allow us to get some idea how our text evolved and who was involved in its creation. Apart from the stone inscriptions and the lamp histories, we have additional sources of great importance for the research of the history of the *Record:* three prefaces written for earlier editions of the *Record* that have not yet been found,[1] and the explanations of 209 difficult terms from the *Record* which are contained in the *Collection of Items from the Garden of the Patriarchs* (Ch. Zutingshiyuan, Jap. Soteijien), a book completed in the year 1108. The explanations of this book refer in sequence to terms contained in an older edition of the *Record,* which is now lost. These and some additional sources make it possible to reconstruct at least part of the history of the *Record.*

Collected Notes

The editorial process of the *Record of Yunmen* took several centuries. Initially, there were some students of Master Yunmen who noted down his words and collected these notes. The older of the two stone inscriptions, written ten years after the master's death, already mentions that "many words [of Yunmen] were written down and circulate in the world."[2] Unfortunately, no source from that period tells us more about the persons who took the notes and their procedure. At the beginning of the twelfth century, the following anecdote was published:

> Chan Master Yunju of Foyin had said:
> When Master Yunmen expounded the Dharma he was like a cloud. He decidedly did not like people to note down his words. Whenever he saw someone doing this he scolded him and chased him out of the hall with the words, "Because your own mouth is not good for anything you come to note down my words. It is certain that some day you'll sell me!"

---

[1] Annotated translations of these prefaces will be included in the edition for specialists (see p. xvi).

[2] See Daijō Tokiwa, *Shina bukkyō shiseki kinenshū,* p. 112.

The History of the *Record of Yunmen*

As to the records of "Corresponding to the Occasion" and "Inside the [Master's] Room":[1] Xianglin and Mingjiao had fashioned robes out of paper and wrote them down immediately whenever they heard them.[2]

Since such stories first appear more than 150 years after Yunmen's death, they are certainly not necessarily reliable. This is especially true in this story, where the two monks mentioned by name became the fathers of two lines within the Yunmen tradition and had successors eager to forge the closest possible link to founding father Yunmen.

Another story, which was already cited in a different context, may be relevant in our search for the note takers; it figures in case 17 (T48: 157a28–b4) of the *Blue Cliff Record,* which appeared in 1128:

Xianglin [Yuan] stayed at Yunmen's side for eighteen years; time and again Yunmen would just call out to him, "Attendant Yuan!" As soon as he responded, Yunmen would say, "What is it?" At such times, no matter how much Xianglin spoke to present his understanding and gave play to his spirit, he never reached mutual accord with Yunmen. One day, though, he suddenly said, "I understand." Yunmen said, "Why don't you say something above and beyond this?" Xianglin stayed on for another three years. A great part of the verbal displays of great ability which Yunmen accorded in his room were designed to make his attendant Yuan able to gain entry and function anywhere. Whenever Yunmen uttered words or a phrase, these were all gathered at attendant Yuan's.

Based on this story, one could assume that the monk called Xianglin (a.k.a. Yuan) was the primary taker of notes. However, in the stone inscription of 959, a man called Shou Jian, not Yuan, is men-

---

[1] "Corresponding to the Occasion" is the title of the main part of the first chapter of the *Record of Yunmen* (T47: 545a16–553b10), and "Inside the [Master's] Room" is part of the title of the first part of the *Record's* second chapter ("Essentials of Words from Inside the [Master's] Room"; T47: 553c24–561c4).

[2] *Linjianlu* (Jap. Rinkanroku), ZZ148: 296b8–12.

tioned as principal attendant of Yunmen. The same name also appears in the colophons to all three fascicles of the oldest extant edition of the *Record of Yunmen* that is stored in Taipei. These colophons say: "Collected by [Master Yunmen's] disciple, Recipient of the Purple [Robe] Shou Jian, [entitled] Grand Master of Clear Knowledge." Unfortunately, very little is known about this man, since his name is otherwise not found in Chan literature. So while we cannot conclusively identify the first note taker(s) and editors, it is likely that they came from the ranks of devoted students of Yunmen who had stayed at his monastery for an extended period of time. Whether it was attendant Yuan, Shou Jian, or some other monk(s) who took the notes and collected them, notes were taken in some form, and one or several followers of Yunmen took charge of collecting and arranging them.

Early Printed Editions

These notes were at some point prepared for being carved in wooden printing blocks. As mentioned above, three prefaces have survived to printed editions that have vanished. These allow the following conclusions: The earliest printed edition of the *Record of Yunmen* probably had already appeared by the year 1035, eighty-six years after the master's death. In the preface to this lost edition, a certain Fuchang Weishan is said to have been the editor of Yunmen's *Record*. Fuchang was a disciple of a successor of Yunmen, Shuangquan Shikuang.

A second edition of the *Record* was prepared by Tianyi Yihuai in 1053, 104 years after Yunmen's death. Unfortunately this edition is also lost except for the preface. The preface, also written by Tianyi, makes it clear that he had an older printed edition as well as several manuscripts at his disposal.

About fifty years later, the learned monk Muan Shanqing also had at least two and possibly more printed editions of Yunmen's records at hand while writing his comments to difficult words entitled *Collection of Items from the Garden of the Patriarchs*. It is possible that his comments concerning the *Record of Yunmen* were keyed to the oldest printed edition. The sequence of the commented words allows the conclusion that Muan's basic text probably contained the first and second fascicles of the *Record of Yunmen* we have today.[1] The choice of translated parts in this volume was partly dictated by the fact that the first and second fascicles appear to be the oldest segments of the *Record*.

Some parts of today's *Record of Yunmen* that go unmentioned in Muan's commentary are cited or at least mentioned in other sources. One can assume that before 1076 about two thirds of today's *Record* were included. Only the first part of fascicle three, i.e., "Critical Examinations," is hardly mentioned. It was probably added in 1076 by Su Xie, the editor in charge of a new printed edition that is the direct ancestor of the edition found in Taipei.

The *Record of Yunmen* edited by Su Xie is also lost, but it is evident from Su Xie's extant preface that his text must have included about 90 percent of the Taipei text of the *Record*. Only a number of poems at the end of the first fascicle and some biographical materials at the end of the third fascicle go unmentioned.

The Oldest Extant Text

The oldest surviving text of the *Record of Yunmen,* which is stored in Taiwan's National Central Library, has colophons which say that a monk named Yuanjue Zongyan was its editor. This monk, who resided on Mt. Gu in Fuzhou province, had in 1144 finished a new edition. Although that edition is lost, we can assume that the 1267 Taipei edition is simply a reproduction of it. Unfortunately we do not know much about Yuanjue Zongyan; he lived from 1074 to 1146 and was a Chan master in the eighth generation of the Yunmen line. He was an important figure as an editor of Chan texts; apart from the *Record of Yunmen,* he also assembled and edited what we now know as the *Record of Linji*. Both records, incidentally, contain a large section entitled "Critical Examinations"; it is likely that in the case of the *Record of Yunmen* this section was assembled and added by Yuanjue person-

---

[1] Muan's comments to the first chapter are congruent with today's first chapter; the second chapter must also have been present, but its two major parts were in reverse order.

ally. The opinions of specialists are divided as to when Yuanjue worked on the *Record of Yunmen:* Seizan Yanagida thinks it was around 1120,[1] but Kōyū Shiina has good reasons to conclude that Yuanjue did this job between 1143 and 1145.[2]

The Taipei edition was printed in 1267 as part of the *Record of the Sayings of Old Worthies* (Ch. Guzunsu yulu; Jap. Kosonshuku goroku). Its printing plates were carved by a certain Wang Yi. Later editions of the *Record of Yunmen* are (with the exception of a few misprints, different colophons, and/or added punctuation) identical with this oldest extant text.

The extant text of the *Record of Yunmen* is, if one compares it with other texts, surprisingly well preserved and documented. Its first two fascicles, from which the majority of text translated in this volume stems, appear to date back to the earliest editions. While we cannot say how closely these correspond to the words said by Master Yunmen, this problem is not unique to the *Record of Yunmen*. The whole "Record of Sayings" literature of Chan Buddhism is in general based on notes by disciples whose accuracy we cannot judge.

But whoever noted down these teachings and however they were edited and arranged, an extraordinary man faces the reader in this text—a man whose words aim, across all differences of time and location and culture and language, at the very heart of being human. My heart. Your heart. Our heart.

---

[1] Seizan Yanagida, "Zenseki kaidai," in *Zenke goroku* vol. 2 (Tokyo: Chikuma shobō, 1974), p. 475. This is to date the most important annotated list of Chan texts.

[2] Kōyū Shiina, "Ummon kōroku to sono shōrokubon no keitō," *Journal of Sōtō Studies* 24 (March 1982), p. 190. This article is the most important Japanese study of the *Record of Yunmen*.

Calligraphy by Shin'ichi Hisamatsu: ''Zen: pointing directly to the human being's heart''

Overview of the Contents of the
Record of Yunmen

■ ■ ■

First Fascicle

*Taishō vol.
47: 544c25–
553c18*

The first fascicle begins with a preface by Su Xie that was written in 1076 for the occasion of the publication of an older, now lost text of the *Record*.

The preface is followed by the main body of the first fascicle, consisting of 320 "cases" of "Responses to Occasions" (545a16–553b10; sections 1 to 144 of this translation). Close to 50 of these are sermons of various length. The rest are exchanges between students and Master Yunmen, usually in the form of short questions by students and pithy answers by Master Yunmen. This is the most important and probably also the oldest part of the *Record*.

The first fascicle closes with the "Songs of the Twelve Time Periods [of the Day]" (553b11–18) and twelve religious verses (553b19–c16).

Second Fascicle

*Taishō vol.
47: 553c20–
567b7*

The second fascicle contains two sections. The first is entitled "Essence of Words from Inside the [Master's] Room" (553c24–561c4; sections 145 to 221 of this translation). In some of the 185 subsections, Master Yunmen teaches his monastic assembly informally at various occasions and places; such instruction is in general less long than his formal sermons in the Dharma Hall and frequently leads rather soon to a question-answer exchange. A great number of subsections in this fascicle feature the master citing words of, anecdotes about, or conversations involving earlier or contemporary masters and monks, and sometimes Buddhist texts. These anecdotes or quotes are usually followed by Yunmen's comments, by questions, or by discussions with his students.

The second section, entitled "Statements with Answers in Place of the Audience" (561c5–567b5; sections 222 to 263 of this translation), contains 290 cases of statements by Master Yunmen. They have different forms and are of varying structure, but all are brought forth with the aim of provoking the audience. As the listeners usually turn out to be unable to respond, Yunmen usually gives one or more responses that express the understanding and thoughts of the audience or his own.

*Taishō vol.
47: 567b9–
576c29*

Third Fascicle

The third and last fascicle consists of six parts and one appendix. The first and most voluminous part is called "Critical Examinations" (567b16–573b3; sections 264 to 277 of this translation); this is a collection of Yunmen's exchanges with many masters, monks, and disciples. Most often, Yunmen confronts them with questions or challenging statements and tries in this manner to provoke expressions of their Chan realization and understanding. This expression is then "critically examined" by the master. Such examinations can take various forms, but most of Yunmen's partners fail this test; the master then often fuels their doubts by stinging remarks or by words and/or actions that either express his own realization and understanding or highlight (the lack of) that of the challenged person.

The second part of the third fascicle is a "Pilgrimage Record" (573b4–575a20; sections 278 to 283 of this translation) in which Yunmen's conversations with many famous masters of the time are recorded. It shows clear traces of later editorial work and is of only limited value for Yunmen's biography.

The remaining parts are relatively brief: the master's testament (575a21–b11), his last instructions (575b12–c2), a biographical record

Overview of the Contents of the *Record of Yunmen*

(575c3–576a18) written by the official Lei Yue on the day of the master's burial (but certainly heavily revised at a much later date), a petition by court officials to the ruler of the Nanhan empire to nominate Yunmen abbot of the Lingshu monastery (576a19–b6), and the story of the opening of Yunmen's stupa seventeen years after his death (576b7–16).

The appendix (576b19–c27) consists of twelve verses by Yunmen's disciple Great Master Yuanming.

Yunmen-Related Koans

. . .

In all major koan collections, koans featuring Master Yunmen are more numerous than those of any other master. The table on the following pages should facilitate looking up koans from the following collections in this translation and vice versa:

1. The *Blue Cliff Record* (Ch. Biyanlu, Jap. Hekiganroku). English translation mentioned in the Selective Bibliography under Cleary.

2. The *Gateless Barrier* (Ch. Wumenguan, Jap. Mumonkan). English translations (with varying titles) are mentioned in the Bibliography under Cleary (1993), Shibayama (1974), and Yamada (1990). Original text: Taishō vol. 48, No. 2005.

3. The *Record of Serenity* (Ch. Congronglu, Jap. Shōyōroku). English translation by Cleary (1990). Original text: Taishō vol. 48, No. 2004.

4. The *Three Hundred Koans* (Jap. Sanbyakusoku) by Dōgen Kigen. No English translation available as of 1993.

Additionally, this table lets practitioners and scholars compare Yunmen–related koans in the listed collections.

Table of Well-known Koans Featuring Yunmen

Transl. section	Record of Yunmen	Blue Cliff Record	Gateless Barrier	Record of Serenity	300 Koans
2	545b2–5	Case 39; 177c5–8			
13	545c7–8	Case 14; 154c2			
26	546a10–11	Case 50; 185b7		Case 99; 291b8–9	Case 158
51	547c4–5				Case 166
58	548b5–6	Case 77; 204b11–12		Case 78; 277b5–6	
85	550b15		Case 21; 295c6		
89	550b24–25	Case 15; 155a21–22			Case 95
92	550c4–6				Case 208
95	550c19–20	Case 27; 167b24–25			
139	552c27–29	Case 39; 177b14–17			
140	553a1–2		Case 16; 295a12–13		
147	554a6–9	Case 34; 172c19–23			
149	554a13–15			Case 82; 280a12–14	Case 257
158	555a3–7		Case 48; 299a2–6	Case 61; 265a21–25	
179	556c29–557a2				Case 176
185	557b25	Case 87; 212a11–12			
186	557b29–c2	Case 8; 148b1–4		Case 71; 272a4–7	

Transl. section	Record of Yunmen	Blue Cliff Record	Gateless Barrier	Record of Serenity	300 Koans
188	557c20–21		Case 39; 297c22–24		
191	558a8–10				Case 72
192	558a14–15	Case 47; 183a17			
193	558a20–25			Case 11; 234a1–8	Case 107
197	558b23–24	Case 60; 192b7–10			
213	560a17–26	Case 88; 212c8–22			
221	561a10–13			Case 21; 240c13–18	
223	561c18–20	Case 83; 208c29–209a2		Case 31; 248a5–7	
243	563b17–18	Case 6; 145c12–14			
245	563b22–24	Case 86; 211b13–16			Case 81
260	556a1–2				Case 162
270	570a21–24	Case 54; 188b19–24			
273	572a23–28		Case 15; 294c24–29		Case 280
280	573c15–20				Case 100
281	574a10–21				Case 285
283	574a26–b1				Case 70
285	574c16–18			Case 40; 253b22–25	

Table of Well-known Koans Featuring Yunmen (Continued)

Transl. section	Record of Yunmen	Blue Cliff Record	Gateless Barrier	Record of Serenity	300 Koans
—	—				Cases 231,261

Selective Bibliography

■ ■ ■

Works of Reference

App, Urs. "Reference Works for Chan Research." *Cahiers d'Extrême-Asie* 7 (1993–94), pp. 357–409.

Demiéville, Paul; May, Jacques; et al. *Hōbōgirin: Dictionnaire encyclopédique du bouddhisme d'après les sources chinoises et japonaises* (Hōbōgirin: Encyclopedic dictionary of Buddhism after the Chinese and Japanese sources). 6 vols. to date. Paris: A. Maisonneuve; Tokyo: Maison Franco-Japonaise, 1927–.

Fischer-Schreiber, Ingrid; Ehrhard, Franz-Karl; and Diener, Michael S. *The Shambhala Dictionary of Buddhism and Zen.* Boston: Shambhala, 1991.

Inagaki, Hisao. *A Glossary of Zen Terms.* Kyoto: Nagata Bunshōdō, 1991. (Reviewed in Urs App, "Zen Glossary on the Quick," *Japanese Religions* 17, no. 1 [January 1992], pp. 75–85.)

Komazawa daigaku nai Zengaku daijiten hensansho (Compilation office at Komazawa University of the large dictionary of Zen studies). *Zengaku daijiten* (Large dictionary of Zen studies). Tokyo: Taishūkan shoten, 1977.

Miura, Isshū, and Sasaki, Ruth Fuller. *Zen Dust.* Kyoto: The First Zen Institute of America in Japan, 1966 (out of print).

Muan Shanqing. *Zuting shiyuan* (Collection of items from the garden of the patriarchs). Zokuzōkyō collection, vol. 113.

Mujaku Dōchū. *Kattō gosen* (Basket of difficult words). Vol. 9B (pp. 868–1100) of *Zengaku sōsho*. Edited by Seizan Yanagida. Kyoto: Chūbun shuppansha, 1979.

―――. *Zenrin shōkisen* (Basket of articles from the Zen tradition). Vol. 9A of *Zengaku sōsho*. Edited by Seizan Yanagida. Kyoto: Chūbun shuppansha, 1979.

Stone Inscriptions

Chen, Shouzhong. *Dahan shaozhou yunmenshan dajue chansi daciyun kuangshen hongming dashi beiming (bingxu)* (Stone inscription [with preface] for the Great Master [entitled] Great Cloud of Compassion and Immense Understanding of Genuine Truth [who lived in] the Dajue Chan temple on Mt. Yunmen in the Great Han [empire's] Shaozhou district) (964). In: *Shina bukkyō shiseki kinenshū* by Daijō Tokiwa, pp. 115–21. Tokyo: Bukkyō shiseki kenkyūkai, 1931.

Lei, Yue. *Dahan shaozhou yunmenshan guangtai chanyuan gu kuangzhen dashi shixingbei (bing xu)* (True nature epitaph [with preface] for the late great master Kuangzhen from Guangtai Chan temple on Mt. Yunmen in the Great Han [empire's] Shaozhou district) (959). In: *Shina bukkyō shiseki kinenshū* by Daijō Tokiwa, pp. 110–15. Tokyo: Bukkyō shiseki kenkyūkai, 1931.

Text Collections

Dainippon zokuzōkyō (Japanese supplement to the Chinese Buddhist canon). Kyoto: Zōkyō shoin, 1905–1912. Abbreviated as ZZ in text notes.

Guzunsu yulu (Record of the sayings of old worthies) Zokuzōkyō collection, vol. 118. (The oldest version of this collection, which also contains the oldest extant version of the *Record of Yunmen*, is stored in the National Central Library in Taipei, Taiwan.)

Takakusu, Junjirō, et al., eds. *Taishō shinshū daizōkyō* (New edition of the Taishō period of the Chinese Buddhist canon). 100 vols. Tokyo: Taishō issaikyō kankōkai, 1924–1932. Abbreviated as T in text notes.

Yanagida, Seizan, ed. *Zengaku sōsho.* 10 vols. to date. Kyoto: Chūbun shuppansha, 1973 ff.

Zen no goroku (Recorded sayings of Chan). 18 vols. to date. Tokyo: Chikuma shobō, 1969–. (A series of Japanese translations of important Chan texts.)

Sources in Asian Languages

Chodang chip (Ch. Zutangji, Jap. Sodōshū, Eng. Collection from the Founder's Halls). Vol. 4 of *Zengaku sōsho.* Edited by Seizan Yanagida. Kyoto: Chūbun shuppansha, 1974.

Iriya, Yoshitaka. *Gensha kōroku* (Comprehensive record of Xuansha). 2 vols. Kyoto: Zenbunka kenkyūjo, 1987–1989.

Jingde chuandenglu (Jingde era record of the transmission of the lamp). Vol. 51, no. 2076, *Taisho shinshu daizokyo.* Edited by Junjirō Takakasu et al. Tokyo: Taishō issaikyō kankōkai, 1924–1932. (Also available as vol. 6 of *Zengaku sōsho.* Edited by Seizan Yanagida. Kyoto: Chūbun shuppansha, 1976.)

Jueguanlun (Treatise on the ceasing of notions). Several Dunhuang manuscripts reproduced in Gishin Tokiwa trans. *A Dialogue on the Contemplation-Extinguished.* Kyoto: The Institute for Zen Studies, 1973.

Shiina, Kōyū. "Ummon kōroku to sono shorokubon no keitō" (The comprehensive record of Yunmen and the transmission of its various manuscripts). *Journal of Sōtō Studies* (Shūgaku kenkyū) 24 (March 1982), pp. 189–196.

Selective Bibliography

Tokiwa, Daijō. *Shina bukkyō shiseki kinenshū* (Commemorative collection on the history of Chinese Buddhism). Tokyo: Bukkyō shiseki kenkyūkai, 1931.

Yanagida, Seizan. "Goroku no rekishi" (The history of the recorded sayings). *Tōhō gakuhō* (Kyoto) 57 (1985), pp. 211–663.

————. *Shoki zenshūshisho no kenkyū* (Collected research on historical sources of early Chan). Kyoto: Hōzōkan, 1967.

————. "Zenseki kaidai" (Bibliography of Chan literature). In *Zenke goroku* (Records of Chan masters), vol. 2, pp. 445–514. Tokyo: Chikuma shobō, 1974.

————. *Zen no Bunka. (Shiryōhen): Zenrinsōboden* (Zen Culture [Materials]: Transmission of treasures of monks of the Chan tradition). Vol. 1. Kyoto: Kyoto daigaku jinbun kagaku kenkyūjo, 1988.

Yunmen guanglu (Comprehensive record of Yunmen; referred throughout this volume as *Record of Yunmen*). Vol. 47, no. 1988, of *Taishō shinshū daizōkyō*. Edited by Junjirō Takakusu et al. Tokyo: Taishō issaikyō kankōkai, 1924–1932. (The oldest extant edition of this text is mentioned under *Guzunsu yulu*.)

Sources in Western Languages

Antinoff, Steven. "The Problem of the Human Person and the Resolution to That Problem in the Religio-Philosophical Thought of the Zen Master Shin'ichi Hisamatsu." Ph.D. diss., Temple University, 1990.

App, Urs. "Facets of the Life and Teaching of Chan Master Yunmen Wenyan (864–949)." Ph.D. diss., Temple University, 1989.

————. "The Making of a Chan Record." *Annual Report from the Institute for Zen Studies* (Zenbunka kenkyūjo kiyō) 17 (1991), pp. 1–90.

Blyth, R. H. *Zen and Zen Classics*. Vol. 2, *History of Zen*. Tokyo: Hokuseido Press, 1976.

Selective Bibliography

Chang, Chung-yuan. *Original Teachings of Chan Buddhism*. New York: Vintage Books, 1971.

Chavannes, Edouard. "Le Royaume de Wou et de Yüeh" (The kingdom of Wu and Yue). *T'oung-pao* 17 (1916), pp. 37–49.

Cleary, Christopher, trans. *Swampland Flowers: The Letters and Lectures of Zen Master Ta Hui*. New York: Grove Press, 1977.

Cleary, Thomas, trans. *Book of Serenity*. Hudson, N.Y.: The Lindisfarne Press, 1990.

———. *No Barrier*. New York: Bantam Books, 1993.

Cleary, Thomas and J. C., trans. *The Blue Cliff Record*. 3 vols. Boulder, Col., and London: Shambhala, 1977.

Conze, Edward. *A Short History of Buddhism*. London: George Allen & Unwin, 1980.

DeMartino, Richard. "The Human Situation and Zen Buddhism." In *Zen Buddhism and Psychoanalysis,* by D. T. Suzuki, E. Fromm, and R. DeMartino, pp. 142–71. New York: Harper & Row, 1970.

———. "On Zen Communication." *Communication 8,* no. 1 (1983), pp. 13–28.

———. "The Zen Understanding of Man." Ph.D. diss., Temple University, 1969.

Dumoulin, Heinrich. *Zen Buddhism: A History*. Vol. 1, *India and China*. New York: Macmillan, 1988.

Gernet, Jacques. *A History of Chinese Civilization*. Cambridge and New York: Cambridge University Press, 1982.

Graham, A. C. *Chuang-tzu: The Inner Chapters*. London: George Allen & Unwin, 1981.

Gundert, Wilhelm. *Bi-yän-lu: Meister Yüan-wu's Niederschrift von der Smaragdenen Felswand* (Biyanlu: Master Yuanwu's record of the emerald cliff). Frankfurt/M: Ullstein Verlag, 1983.

Selective Bibliography

Hisamatsu, Shin'ichi. "The Characteristics of Oriental Nothingness." *Philosophical Studies of Japan* 2 (1960), pp. 65–97.

―――. *Zen and the Fine Arts.* New York and Tokyo: Kodansha International, 1974.

Lamotte, Étienne. *L'Enseignement de Vimalakīrti* (The teaching of Vimalakīrti). Louvain, Belgium: Institut Orientaliste, 1962.

―――. *History of Indian Buddhism.* Louvain, Belgium: Peeters Press, 1988.

Lu, K'uan-yü [Charles Luk]. *Ch'an and Zen Teachings, Second Series.* London: Rider, 1961.

Morinaga, Sōkō. *A Treatise on the Ceasing of Notions.* Translated by Ursula Jarand. London: The Zen Centre, 1988.

Plessner, Helmuth. *Die Stufen des Organischen und der Mensch* (The stages of the organic and man). Berlin: de Gruyter, 1965.

Sasaki, Ruth Fuller. *The Recorded Sayings of Ch'an Master Lin-chi Hui-chao of Chen Prefecture.* Kyoto: The Institute for Zen Studies, 1975.

Sasaki, Ruth Fuller; Iriya, Yoshitaka; and Fraser, Dana R. *The Recorded Sayings of Layman P'ang.* New York and Tokyo: Weatherhill, 1971.

Schafer, Edward H. *The Empire of Min.* Rutland, Vt., and Tokyo: Tuttle, 1954.

―――. "The History of the Empire of Southern Han." In *Silver Jubilee Volume of the Zinbun Kagaku Kenkyūsyo.* Kyoto: Institute for Humanistic Studies of Kyoto University, 1954.

Shibayama, Zenkei. *Zen Comments of the Mumonkan.* New York: Mentor Books, 1974.

Sørensen, Henrik Hjort. "The Life and Times of the Ch'an Master Yün-men Wen-yen." *Acta orientalia 49,* pp. 105–31.

Sprung, Mervyn, ed. *The Problem of Two Truths in Buddhism and Vedanta*. Dordrecht, Netherlands: Reidel, 1973.

Suzuki, Daisetz T. *Essays in Zen Buddhism (First Series)*. New York: Harper & Brothers, 1949.

———. *Essays in Zen Buddhism (Second Series)*. London: Rider & Co., 1974.

———. *Manual of Zen Buddhism*. New York: Grove Press, 1978.

Tokiwa, Gishin, trans. *A Dialogue on the Contemplation-Extinguished*. Kyoto: The Institute for Zen Studies, 1973.

Waddell, Norman, trans. *The Unborn: The Life and the Teaching of Zen Master Bankei*. San Francisco: North Point Press, 1984.

Watson, Burton, trans. *The Complete Works of Chuang Tzu*. New York: Columbia University Press, 1968.

Wu, John C. H. *The Golden Age of Zen*. Taipei: United Publishing Center, 1975.

Yamada, Kōun. *The Gateless Gate*. Tucson: University of Arizona Press, 1990.

Yampolsky, Philip. *The Platform Sutra of the Sixth Patriarch*. New York: Columbia University Press, 1967.

Yanagida, Seizan. "The 'Recorded Sayings' Texts of Chinese Ch'an Buddhism." In *Early Ch'an in China and Tibet,* edited by Whalen Lai and Lewis R. Lancaster. Berkeley: University of California, 1983.